Reactive Attachment Disorder 101

A Guidebook for Parents Raising Children and Teenagers with Reactive Attachment Disorder (RAD)

Esther Bernstein

contained within this document, including, but not limited to, errors, omissions, or inaccuracies.

Table of Contents

Introduction

"The kids who need the most love will ask for it in the most unloving ways."

—by Russell Barkley

Image 1: Happy Children

The bond between a parent and child is one of the most beautiful relationships in the human experience. There is very little a child can do to break the bond. From the other angle, in the first years of life, children are entirely devoted to strengthening that connection. It is this expectation, however, that makes it so completely devastating when your child does not exhibit this desire to bond.

I have spent the last five years of my life studying various behavioral disorders in children, including Reactive Attachment Disorder (RAD), in order to assist families struggling with the effects. For me, this journey has not just been a professional one, but a personal one too. When my son, Craig, was diagnosed with RAD I was stunned, but I also felt relieved. At last, I had an answer as to why I could not forge a bond with my child. We could finally move forward and start to heal. At the time of the diagnosis, my life was a daily dose of hell, although I would only realize that later. My husband and I became so used to living with the issues of RAD that we no longer lived. We just existed from moment to moment with this little boy that wanted nothing to do with us.

Throughout the years, as we started to heal and I became more involved with other families living with RAD, I felt a deep desire to help others in the same situation. The techniques we learned from our psychiatrist were invaluable, but it was the small things that we learned by actually parenting a child with RAD that I really want to share.

The root of my son's trauma was in very early infanthood and it did not involve significant, consistent abuse. As a result, it was far easier for us to make progress once we understood his condition. I would later learn through my work that this is not the case for many families. Whether a child is biological or adopted has no bearing on a RAD diagnosis. Many children with RAD have lived through significant trauma and caring for a child with multiple issues is exhausting and emotionally draining at times. I understand this at a deep level. It is my intention that, by writing this book and sharing my personal experience and professional expertise, I will be able to reignite hope in the heart of the parent of a RAD child.

Medicating a RAD child is a controversial topic. In most cases, medication is a purely personal choice. In severe cases, where the child is a danger to themselves and others, medication may be necessary to guarantee the physical safety of the family unit. We had Craig medicated for a very short period, but eventually determined that it was not the right choice for our family. In the families I've interacted with, some felt similarly, but there are also those that felt medication was their only solution. As in any psychiatric condition, medication always needs to be paired with psychotherapy and proper coping mechanisms ensure the child is able to move forward. While it is important to always follow the advice of the medical and psychiatric team treating your child, in this book, I hope to provide more options for parents of RAD children so that they do not feel like medication is their only route.

The most important part of this journey for me was learning everything I could about RAD. This interest turned into a career for me, but it doesn't need to go that far for you. Knowledge really is power and when you are able to understand exactly what your child is dealing with and why, you will be far better equipped to help them and yourself.

Although my son was very young when he was in the throes of this disorder, through my work I have also learned how to deal with teenage children with RAD. Teenagers come with the whole added issue of hormonal changes and peer pressure which can make dealing with RAD far more difficult. I will share teenager-specific advice with you that I've managed to gather throughout the years.

Whenever you deal with a disorder of any kind, you suddenly have experts popping up all over the place. Anyone and everyone seems to have advice. As a result, many myths arise. This has been the case with RAD too. In this book, I hope to dispel these myths so that the truth about this disorder can prevail and we can help our children to move forward.

At the end of the day, expert advice is important. There are men and women that have studied this and other behavioral disorders for many years in a psychiatric capacity and they have a lot to add in terms of raising RAD children. These people spend a small amount of time with your child, though, and you spend almost every waking hour living with and fighting against RAD. It's, therefore, vital to gain perspective from other parents that are living with the same situation and acknowledge that, despite the fact that these people lack professional qualifications, their experience is equally important.

Chapter 1:

Understanding Reactive

Attachment Disorder

The first sign that Craig was dealing with something deeper than simple behavioral issues came quite early. He was about nine months old and a very independent baby. My friends would comment about how content he was to play on his own, and how he wasn't particularly clingy like many babies his age. While they all thought it wonderful that he could occupy himself for long periods of time with his toys on the lounge floor, I didn't feel great about it. I told myself that I was being silly. I just wanted my baby to seek me out the way others' infants did. I really did my best to convince myself that this was a good thing. Craig was independent and happy to be on his own. I should be grateful for that.

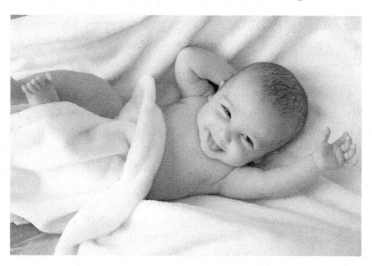

Image 2: Young baby

As he began to grow, and we spent more time around other people, it was clear that this wasn't just a case of an independent baby. Craig had never been a particularly affectionate child. My husband and I never saw the sweet, cherubic, open-mouthed kisses that babies give before they learn to smooch their lips together. In fact, Craig soon started to act up and wail when either of us picked him up. With strangers, though, he was a different child entirely. He would run up to adults he had never met before and throw his little arms around their legs. They thought it was cute. I was horrified. My little boy who had never shown any affection to his parents was quite content to interact with complete strangers. I cannot explain the devastation of those early years to you. I was convinced my child hated me and his father. I feared we did something to turn him against us.

Believing we simply had to try harder, we muddled on as best we could. My relationship with my husband suffered as we disagreed on how to handle the situation. Not once did it cross our minds that there was a diagnosable condition at work.

When Craig started kindergarten, the teacher contacted us from almost the first day. Craig would swing the pendulum between inappropriate affection—throwing his arms around other children in the middle of class without warning—and aggression towards his classmates. At most times, he refused to answer his teacher directly. He would either completely ignore her or give the answer to another child instead of answering her.

His aggression and refusal to obey the rules increased at home as well. When we had our second child, Miley, our home situation got to the point where I actually feared for the safety of my newborn. It wasn't that I thought Craig would intentionally hurt her, but when he was in the throes of a tantrum, it was very difficult to control his angry outbursts.

The first time I heard the term 'Reactive Attachment Disorder' was not in a psychologist or psychiatrist's office. It was actually at a dinner party. We had taken a rare night off to join our friends at their home to celebrate a birthday. My mom was caring for the children that night, and we were about halfway through the main meal when we got a call. It was my mother calling to ask where the diapers were kept. Craig had dumped all of Miley's diapers from the drawer into the bathtub when she had told him it was bathtime. I sighed and apologized to her, directing her to the hall cupboard where we kept the spare packs. When I ended the call, I realized my husband started sharing some of Craig's other behaviors. At first, I was a little annoyed. We generally did not talk about Craig's behavior with others. I was sure that it would make us look like bad parents. One person at the table was taking particular interest, though, and I would be forever grateful that my husband had broken our code of silence.

Mabel worked as a private social worker, and often dealt with children in the foster and adoption system. She asked me if Craig was our biological child, to which I answered that he was. She carefully weighed her words before asking, "Have you ever had to be separated from Craig, when he was an infant perhaps?"

My heart sunk. Later on, I found that she held back on asking if there had been any abuse in Craig's past, understandably realizing that would not be the best dinner table conversation. Thankfully, she had asked just the right question.

I had been separated from Craig when he was just two weeks old. In fact, for the first two months of his life, I had been in and out of hospital. The pregnancy triggered intense high blood pressure, which had not corrected itself, and I had a mild stroke at the age of 29. While I had struggled to live, my husband had been understandably devastated, believing that he was going to lose his wife with no idea how to care for a two week old child alone. Craig was never neglected and my husband did the best he could with a string of *au pairs* and nannies to care for him, but some of these people were better than others. I would later learn my husband fired one after coming home to find Craig screaming in a filthy diaper in his crib and the young girl in the backyard smoking a cigarette.

I don't think I ever really dealt with the guilt I felt about that period in my son's life. Although I did my best to make up for it, I also never thought it had anything to do with the behavioral problems he exhibited later on. After hearing our story, Mabel suggested we see a particular psychiatrist that she often used for the children she worked with in the foster care system. A birthday dinner and a desperate phone call had finally set us all on the path to healing.

What Is Reactive Attachment Disorder?

So what exactly is Reactive Attachment Disorder (RAD)? Very simply, it is a serious, but rare, condition in which a child is unable to establish healthy attachments to primary caregivers or parents. Where the study of psychiatry is concerned, RAD falls under the umbrella of attachment disorders that develop in young children who struggle to form emotional attachments to others. In this context, attachment is defined as the deep connection that normally forms between a child and the person responsible for their care. This connection is encoded into the brain of a young child during the early years of development (Mayo Clinic, 2017b).

According to Maslow's Hierarchy of Needs, a well-known tabulation used to determine the importance levels of various needs in the lives of human beings, attachment to a loving parent or caregiver that provides love, support, and guidance is a very basic human need. If this need is not met or unable to be accepted, human beings will struggle to meet many other levels of needs. RAD generally lasts a lifetime, but children or adolescents that are diagnosed with the disorder can be taught to develop healthy and stable relationships with parents and caregivers through a treatment program.

What Causes Reactive Attachment Disorder?

RAD has been known to develop if a child's basic need for affection, comfort, and nurturing are not met and stable, loving, and caring attachments are not established. When a child's emotional needs are not met or they are ignored, they learn not to expect comfort or care from a caregiver and therefore do not establish an emotional connection with them.

Examples of this withholding of care in infancy can include a baby that is left in a soiled diaper for many hours; a baby that is not fed for extended periods, left to cry or not comforted when it is distressed; and also when the baby is not interacted with, spoken to, touched, or held for many hours. There are many other instances in which babies may develop RAD through withholding of care (Mayo Clinic, 2017b).

It is important to note that not all infants that experience such withholding of care, neglect, or outright abuse will develop RAD. We also do not yet know why some children develop the disorder while others with the same experiences do not.

Risk Factors for Developing RAD

There are certain groups of children that are at higher risk for developing this and other behavioral disorders. This includes children that live in institutional settings or children's homes; children that frequently change caregivers or foster homes; children of caregivers that are involved in criminal activity, abuse substances, or have severe mental health problems; where parents are separated from their children for prolonged periods due to hospitalization or imprisonment; and also when the child has experienced multiple traumatic losses very early in life (Mayo Clinic, 2017b).

It must be noted that most children that are severely neglected do not develop RAD.

Symptoms of RAD

Image 3: Fearful child

While symptoms of RAD are particular to the child in question, their personality, experiences, and ordinary reactions to trauma, there are a few symptoms that are frequently found in children with the disorder. This is by no means a tool for diagnosis. Attempting self-diagnosis of RAD is not only extremely irresponsible, but also not helpful to the child. Some of the symptoms often seen in children before the age of five with RAD include:

- Unexplained fearfulness, sadness, withdrawal from social or family interactions, or irritability
- Listless and sad appearance
- An apparent fear of their caretakers where this fear does not seem to be warranted
- Failure to seek comfort or a lack of response when comfort is provided
- The child seldom smiles
- The child watches others closely, but refuses to engage in social situations
- Failure to ask for assistance or support
- The child does not reach for the caregiver when they are picked up
- No enjoyment of interactive or engaging games
- The child takes a long time to calm down after they become upset
- The child does not seek out comfort from their caregiver when they are upset
- Little to no emotion is apparent when interacting with others
- The child may report feeling alone or unsafe
- The child exhibits control issues and anger problems
- The child has difficult showing genuine affection and care
- An aversion to physical affection or touch (Mayo Clinic, 2017b).

Development of RAD Symptoms

As a child with RAD grows older, their symptoms will usually begin to fall into one of two general categories: inhibited RAD and disinhibited RAD (WebMD, 2020).

In inhibited RAD, children are aware of what happens around them, but they often do not respond to external stimuli such as being asked a question or someone calling their name. Inhibited RAD children may also be withdrawn, emotionally unresponsive, and have a tendency to keep to themselves, even in the family home. They will generally not seek or show affection to caregivers and seem to have no desire to interact with others (WebMD, 2020).

In contrast, disinhibited RAD is when children are over friendly with strangers and display inappropriate familiarity or abnormal selection in those they attach themselves to. Disinhibited RAD children often do not prefer their caregivers over strangers or people that they do not know well and, in many cases, behave immaturely for their age and seek out affection in unsafe ways (WebMD, 2020).

These symptoms can come with an entire set of complications in mental and physical health which are linked to the disorder. Developmental milestones may be delayed in RAD children, and there may also be delays in physical growth. The latter is often linked to eating difficulties. Emotional issues such as anxiety, depression, eating disorders, and anger management difficulties may also arise as a result of RAD. In older children, drug and alcohol abuse and dependencies are not uncommon and learning or behavioral issues at school may exacerbate the emotional difficulties they are experiencing.

It is rather common for older RAD children and adults with RAD to have difficulty in maintaining relationships, both with friends and romantic partners. As adults, they will often change jobs frequently and be unemployed for long periods. As RAD children age, especially if they show disinhibited symptoms, inappropriate sexual behavior may also emerge as well as low self esteem and delinquent or anti social behaviors (WebMD, 2020).

Complications of RAD

Without treatment, RAD can continue for many years and may have lifelong consequences.

Some research indicates that some teenagers and children with RAD may display callous, unemotional traits that can include behavior problems and cruelty toward animals or people. More research is needed, however, to determine if problems in older children and adults are related to experiences of RAD in early childhood (Cleveland Clinic, 2018).

Possible Prevention

While it's not known definitively if RAD can be prevented, there may be ways to reduce the risk of it developing. Young children and infants need a stable, caring environment and their basic physical and emotional needs must be consistently met. Some of these suggestions may help:

- Volunteer or take classes with children if you lack experience or skill with babies or children. This will help you learn how to interact with them in a nurturing manner.
- Be actively engaged with your child by lots of talking, playing, eye contact, and smiling.
- Learn to interpret your infant's cues, such as different types of cries, so that you can meet their needs quickly and effectively.
- Provide nurturing and warm interaction with your child, such as during feeding, bathing or changing of diapers.

- Offer both verbal and nonverbal responses to the child's feelings through facial expressions, touch, and tone of voice (Cleveland Clinic, 2018).

How is RAD Diagnosed?

RAD is not usually diagnosed before nine months of age. Diagnosis will best be made by a pediatric psychiatrist or psychologist by conducting a thorough, and in-depth examination. This may help to diagnose RAD as well as any other disorders which may coexist (Mayo Clinic, 2017a).

According to the *Diagnostic and Statistical Manual of Mental Disorders* (5th ed; DSM-5), a manual for the diagnosis and assessment of mental disorders from the American Psychiatric Association, the diagnostic criteria for RAD include the presence of consistently withdrawn emotional behavior toward caregivers including not seeking out or responding to comfort when distressed. Another diagnostic criteria is the presence of persistent emotional and social problems including difficulties in responding to others, no positive response to social interaction, and unexplained sadness, fearfulness, or irritability when dealing with caregivers. RAD diagnostic criteria also include a persistent lack of emotional need for stimulation, comfort, and affection from caregivers as well as a frequent change of caregivers which gives the child little chance to form stable connections. This could also be identified in a care situation where many children are cared for by few caregivers and there is little chance for the child to receive sufficient individual attachment. Diagnostic criteria for RAD often depends on the child not having a diagnosis of autism spectrum disorder as the diagnostic criteria regularly overlap (APA, 2013).

Methods of evaluation for RAD may include direct observation of the way a child interacts with its parents or caregivers. Evaluators may also look at patterns of behavior and examples of the child's interactions and responses in a variety of situations. There will also be a range of questions that caregivers or parents will need to answer about the home and the living situation since birth. Although it may be difficult for parents and caregivers to provide, often very personal, accounts of issues which could be emotional, it is vital to deliver this information in the most honest and clear way possible. Your child's future may depend upon it. Evaluation will also include the parenting style and ability and while this can also be difficult feedback to get, it is important to try to take it onboard and not become defensive. There is, after all, no manual to parenting and no one teaches you how to be a parent. We can all do better and if we can learn how to improve our parenting skills we should embrace the opportunity (Mayo Clinic, 2017a).

Your child's doctor will also want to rule out other psychiatric disorders and determine if any other mental health conditions co-exist, such as:

- Depressive disorders
- Intellectual disability
- Autism spectrum disorder
- Other adjustment disorders

Real Life Situation

I've chosen to include this particular real life story in the book as it illustrates the sometimes difficult road that parents walk to a RAD diagnosis. It is not always a linear journey, and often this has to do with the parents' own difficulty to take the diagnosis on board.

Sally says that she wrote her story several times in her head and on the computer, before she eventually got it out, each time it was a completely different story. At first she wondered how a description of the same situation could vary so much from one day to the next and then she remembered, it is because RAD kids are different each day.

Each day is a bit of a mystery, she says, and she never really knows how her daughter, Amber, will act or react to her, her siblings, complete strangers or even acquaintances.

When Sally and her husband first began adopting, she thought the one disability she could not handle was a cognitive disability. She now knows how wrong she was. She now feels that she has been blessed with two children living with cognitive disabilities and other children with learning challenges, and they could not feel more grateful to be the parents of the children that were chosen for their family. In her opinion, their special needs are completely manageable and they are a wonderful addition to her family. Today, she could not imagine her life without them, but things have not always been that easy.

As Sally and her husband got further down the adoption road, they started hearing about families that had children with Reactive Attachment Disorder, commonly referred to as RAD. Sally felt bad for "them." She would read those families' stories, they were heartbreaking and being parents in such a situation seemed so challenging. Sally knew then that RAD would be a very difficult disorder for her to deal with and she hoped that they would never see it.

Shortly after that, Sally, with a wry smile, says that they were blessed with a child that experienced a difficult settling-in period and integrating into their family. At first, Sally thought Amber was just strong willed, hurt, and confused. She believed all they had to do was allow her enough time and she would settle in on her own. Perhaps it would be a couple of months or even a year. With their other adoptions, time had been an important factor in healing. As time passed by, first months and then years, Sally could see that something wasn't quite right. She didn't want to admit that she thought her child suffered from RAD. She admits now that she was in denial.

Over the almost four years that Amber lived with Sally's family, they became terrifyingly aware that Amber definitely suffered from this attachment disorder. Her behaviors and symptoms were classic RAD behaviors. She admits that it did help them to have a name for what they were seeing and what they couldn't understand or explain. It was not what Sally wanted in an adoption experience, but it is what it is, and at least now they know what they are dealing with.

At first, Sally says she took it personally. She asked herself all the usual questions:

What was she doing wrong?

Why couldn't Amber bond to her?

Was she really that unlovable?

Would Amber do better with another family?

What does she need to do to facilitate bonding?

Why does Amber do these inexplicable things?

Why are Amber's actions and behaviors so different from those of the other children?

Why does Sally feel confused and why is she starting to question herself?

Why does she sometimes think they are doing pretty good and then other times think they just seemed to relapse completely?

RAD can develop in any child. It is not just foster children or older child adoption that are at risk for this disorder. It is caused by a combination of their individual personality and their past experiences as well as their personal coping skills. Raging hormones in teenagers can also make RAD even more difficult to deal with.

A child living with this disorder finds it extremely difficult to trust anyone, and this extends to the child's adoptive parents. Sally feels that RAD is a very sad condition because it steals the child's childhood. These children have already been so hurt by life and the disorder takes away any chance of happiness outside of the abusive situation as well. It affects the life they live with their new family and even their adulthood, in some cases. If they are unable to bond with their adoptive parents, they may well struggle to bond to a significant other, spouse, friend, or their future child.

As Sally's situation became painfully obvious, she approached a friend who was also a social worker, worked with adoption organizations, and was a parent of an adopted child herself. Sally knew that her friend had the knowledge they needed regarding RAD, teenagers, and adoption. Sally's friend was able to help their family by providing them with factual information on RAD and helping them develop plans to handle certain situations. As Sally read the articles she felt that they were describing her daughter. She realized that she was not imagining things or losing her mind and other parents struggle with the same behaviors from their RAD child. She was not alone.

Sally says that if you think your child may have RAD, you should not be scared to ask for answers to your questions and look for the support and help you need. She says that parents should not hesitate to make contact with their social worker, get in touch with other families living with RAD children, make use of support groups they will find on the internet, join adoption support groups in the community, attend conferences about parenting, or consult a therapist that is specifically trained in Reactive Attachment Disorder.

Sally says that if you are having difficulty in your ongoing adoption, do some research into RAD and consider whether it could be the cause of the difficulties. Occasionally, RAD symptoms are hidden in the beginning phase of adjustment. Don't be ashamed to admit that your child is living with this disorder and definitely do not blame yourself. The child is simply a victim of what happened to them and they need help to move past it. To be able to give them that help, you will need tools and support to make it possible.

Sally has found that her first instinctive reaction when interacting with a child that has RAD is not always the best reaction. When reacting to her daughter's behaviors, she needs to take a step back and remember that she is a victim of her disorder. She is not purposefully trying to be hurtful to Sally. The coping skills she developed, if any, are extremely limited and childlike. She oftentimes is stuck in survival mode. Sally knows that she needs to be the grown-up and her own reactions need to be helpful in moving her daughter toward comfort, trust, and security.

She acknowledges that she certainly doesn't have it all figured out at this point and would definitely say that they are still a work in progress.

In the fall of 2015, Sally and her family attended the Empowered to Connect conference. They were able to embrace and resonate with the theory that backed up the recommended parenting techniques. Sally wondered if she was personally capable of implementing it with her children 24 hours a day, seven days a week. She was encouraged when she heard about the concept of "do-overs." She was more hopeful when she learned that the techniques can be done just 30% of the time to have a significant impact on the child.

When Sally visualizes what she wants for her daughter and their challenges, she can picture how, by working with these strategies, one would see excellent results with a RAD child. She is doing it now, but as with many things, results take time to become evident. Sally acknowledges that there is no instruction manual to heal a child with this disorder. It will only be with a combination of acceptance, patience, providing security, unconditional love, and simply being there for her daughter that she will stay on track to healing.

Sally understands first hand that if you have a child with RAD, you know that this is not in any way easy. It is one of the most difficult things you will ever experience in your life. RAD children will push you away and refuse any offer of help or kindness. This is because they are so badly hurt, deeply afraid, and unable to trust. It is certainly not the type of situation that makes a parent want to repeat the experience. If anything it will have you recoiling in horror. Sally says that if you are anything like her, and many other parents, you will understand that you have no other choice but to be better than you really are. It is so vital that you do everything you can to attempt to create a lasting bond of trust with your child.

Sally finds herself needing a moment to meditate and process daily. There are many feelings running through her head, but she ultimately comes back to the fact that Amber is a very hurt child and currently she is not a hurt adult. So she swallows her pride, her insecurities, and her opinions and she "goes back for more." Why? Because Amber deserves whatever help and love she can give her.

Once Sally and her family understood what was going on with their daughter, they needed to take things and people out of their life that were harming their bonding process. For their child's future mental health, they needed to be the most important people in her life. This is not for the purposes of an ego boost but, instead, it is for her future ability to bond, trust, and heal. They could not allow anyone else to be in that coveted position in her life. It did not matter whether it was babysitters, family members, previous teachers, friends with good intentions, or anyone else for that matter. These people first needed to be educated and if that didn't work then they needed to be removed from the equation, if possible. Sally says that, as a parent of a RAD child, for your own emotional well-being, you should not listen to others who make unkind comments, assumptions, or place judgment on you. Their words are not helpful when you already do your best to navigate an extremely challenging parenting situation.

Sally found that humor is a vital medicine for RAD families. It is part of healing, it is important, and it is fun. Sally and the members of her family try to have fun, joke, be joyful, and laugh with their children as much as they can. Humor seems to be an anxiety and stress reducer for her child with RAD. They try not to react in a way that could ultimately hurt her and them during critical situations. What feels like a good reaction to a situation in the moment, is often not always the most beneficial reaction when dealing with a RAD child.

Sally and her family have started to make a point of verbally reassuring their daughter that they love her and that they are there for her. They want her to hear it as much as possible so that she will, hopefully, start to believe it. When she is not kind to them or her siblings, they let her know that they love her, but that they do not necessarily love the way she is treating her siblings, acting, or that they are not onboard with a decision that she may have made. Sally admits that it is much easier said than done.

Sally hopes to do all that she can do for her child with RAD, but she knows that she needs to remember that there are other children in the family, too. Sometimes they get caught in the crossfire of emotions and that just doesn't seem fair. As they attempt to help their daughter, they feel it is equally important to nurture and enjoy their other children. They don't want to over focus on unhealthy behaviors but instead have the main focus of their family be all that is good and healthy. A RAD child may attempt to bring you and their siblings down with them. It is Sally's plan to not go down together. She wants to try to help Amber without the rest of her family being harmed. Sometimes difficult decisions need to be made and she hopes not to be in that situation. If they are, she says, they will make whatever decision is best for everyone involved.

Sally knows that the overwhelming question is always: how will a child with RAD turn out? Her answer is that there are no guarantees in life, there never has been, and there never will be. Her goal is to do the best she can and hope and pray that it will work. She acknowledges that she can't do anything more than that. She wants to give her child her best effort and the best chance possible toward a healthy, faithful, productive future.

Sally says she is sharing her story in the hope that it will help other families that may find themselves in a similar situation. Although RAD was not what she had planned, it is what she was given (Jean, 2016).

Sally's story highlights how difficult it can be to accept the diagnosis of RAD in your child. For her, previous adoption experiences, although not necessarily easy, were completely different from what she experienced with Amber. She spent a long time believing that what worked with her other children would work with this new child too. This is an interesting perspective for me, because it shows that even experienced parents can completely play it wrong when it comes to a RAD child. As Sally quite rightly says, there is no playbook for dealing with a RAD child, but acceptance of the diagnosis, and taking on board professional advice is your best starting point.

Myths About RAD

As with many emotional, behavioral, or mental disorders several myths have formed around RAD, its causes, and forms of treatment. During my own journey, I came across many pseudo experts that had opinions. Thankfully, I always followed our family psychiatrist's advice and paid little heed to the myths and quick fixes spewed by those with no knowledge about the condition. As a parent, though, desperation can result in believing some of these myths. It is therefore important to be able to identify these.

One of the first myths I came across was that if neglect or abuse causes RAD then love will "cure" it. There are so many reasons that this is not true. In many cases, the caregiver of the RAD child did not cause the disorder, and by the very nature of the disorder, love is rejected by the child. Even parents like me, that found themselves in unavoidable situations that did contribute to my child developing RAD, cannot "love" them better. If love was all it took to heal my son, he would not have RAD (Discovery Mood & Anxiety Program, 2019b).

I also cannot count the number of times that I was told that my son would grow out of his RAD. Of course, this was always by people that were completely ignorant of the realities of the disorder. It is not only hurtful for people to minimize the seriousness of the disorder, but also extremely dangerous to promote this idea. Human beings do not grow out of disorders. If anything, they get worse without treatment and with a disorder like RAD, this means that the child will continue to have poor relationships throughout their life. In fact, it will impact their emotional development to such an extent, if they do not receive treatment, that they could be left with a toddler-like emotional perspective forever. In adults, untreated RAD could lead to a wide range of personality disorders as well.

During my work with children in foster and adoptive homes, another myth that pervaded was that the child just needed a stable and safe home with good morals, and they would settle in time. While this may be true for behavior related solely to trauma, neglect, or abuse which has not resulted in a disorder, this is not true for RAD. The very nature of RAD is that the more the caregiver or parent attempts to provide stability, love, and structure, the more the child will push against that and sabotage their own success. No matter how much time passes, this will not change the instinctive survival mechanisms built into RAD children. In contrast, the more time that passes without treatment, the more likely it is that these behaviors will become entrenched in the child, making healing far more difficult (Discovery Mood & Anxiety Program, 2019b).

I was very lucky when I was seeking out a therapist for my son. The person that identified the behavior was involved with several specialized attachment therapists, so, from the start, we were able to have him treated by the right type of psychiatrist. Throughout the years, I have come to realize that this is not everyone's experience and, often, parents of children with RAD waste valuable time going to a bunch of therapists that were referred by their friends and family. Taking nothing away from the professionalism of these people, they are often not set up or trained to deal with cases of RAD. The psychiatrist or psychologist you see must be experienced in dealing with attachment disorders. Unless their children also have attachment disorders, you can ignore referrals from your friends (Elevations, n.d.).

The next myth about RAD that I want to bust is one that I had to deal with myself, and that is the belief that it is impossible for a child to be traumatized by something that occurred in their pre-verbal phase. My son was just a few months old when I was hospitalized. Because he was so young, when people started to ask about trauma, neglect, or separation in his past, that situation did not immediately cross my mind. In fact, when it happened, I recall comforting myself with the thought that he was so little and wouldn't remember. Little did I know that although he may not recall the exact specifics of the event in his conscious mind, it had already indelibly scarred his subconscious. I would learn throughout my work with children living with behavior disorders that pre-verbal trauma can be even more damaging than post-verbal trauma, predominantly because the child has no way of understanding the situation or expressing their pain. They are trapped in a situation that they have no tools to deal with and no way to escape from. When we look at it from that perspective, it seems completely understandable that a child would be deeply traumatized during this pre-verbal period (Elevations, n.d.).

Another misconception around RAD is that only adopted children present with it. Clearly, my situation alone proves that this is not true. Any event that causes the child to have consistent care withheld can cause RAD to develop, regardless of whether the child is with its biological parents or not (Elevations, n.d.).

Possibly the most damaging myth around RAD is that it is untreatable. If caught early, it is entirely possible to treat this disorder to the point that it has very little impact on the child or the family. Regardless of the age at which RAD is diagnosed, if treatment is comprehensive and sustained, there is every possibility that significant progress can be made. The reason I think this myth is the most damaging of all is that, at the point of diagnosis, parents and caregivers have already been so significantly beaten down emotionally by coping with the behaviors that telling them there is no hope of recovering is like pulling away their last thread of salvation. Parents and caregivers need to understand the true possibilities of recovery for their child in order to fully engage in treatment and care as this will make all the difference.

Flash Myths and Supporting Statistics

Myth: Problems with attachment rarely occur and are not that serious.

Fact: Although RAD is not as collective as other childhood disorders, it is linked to children who have a history of trauma and can have a significant effect on the child's development.

Some Statistics:

- Among children who have experienced neglect, abuse, or both, between 87% and 95% of those children display an insecure attachment.
- A 2006 CDC study showed that one out of 50 infants under one year old in the U.S., based on reports of maltreatment, were submitted to Child Protective Services at some time.
- Attachment disorders were identified by researchers in nearly two-thirds of children in foster care and up to 20% of those living in homeless shelters.
- Of the one million children in the U.S. adopted internationally, or through foster care, 15% (150,000) have severe behavioral problems contributed to attachment and trauma issues; another 30% (300,000) show "some" attachment and behavioral problems worthy of clinical treatment (Discovery Mood & Anxiety Program, 2019b).

Myth: My child was too young to remember.

Fact: Pre-verbal emotional trauma runs very deep and is lasting.

According to the DSM-5, symptoms of RAD must be evident before five years of age, and the child must have a developmental period of at least nine months. The earlier the trauma occurs, the worse it can be carried out later into childhood. Even if your youth is unable to walk or speak, they are still prone to the long-lasting effects of early trauma (Discovery Mood & Anxiety Program, 2019b).

Myth: This child seems perfectly reasonable to me when we are out in public.

Fact: Children with RAD are most likely to act out towards their parents or caretakers and act normal in the presence of strangers.

Children with RAD often do not act anywhere near the same with others as they do with their parents or caregivers. They can be very charming and polite to others. By its very nature, a disorder of attachment means that the child will have the hardest time feeling safe with the people trying to be the most intimate with him/her, such as the parents. If you know this child casually, you're not a threat (Discovery Mood & Anxiety Program, 2019b).

Myth: Reactive attachment disorder can be treated with medication.

Fact: There is no medication for reactive attachment disorder.

Specific parenting patterns in conjunction with professional psychological therapy are the first-line approach to helping a child cope with attachment disorders. The three therapeutic ingredients for a child to develop new patterns of emotional attachment are security, stability, and sensitivity. The primary caregiver must practice extreme patience and give ample time for the child to express his or her emotions. Boundaries must be set but in a loving and empathetic fashion and a stable and repetitive everyday routine must be practiced for the child to regain trust and normalcy in their life (Discovery Mood & Anxiety Program, 2019b).

Chapter Takeaways

- **Definition:** Reactive Attachment Disorder (RAD) is a rare, but serious, condition in which an infant or young child doesn't establish healthy attachments with parents or caregivers.

- **Causes:** RAD most commonly develops when a child's basic needs for comfort, affection and nurturing aren't met and loving, caring, stable attachments with others are not established.
- **Risk Factors:** early trauma including abuse and neglect for various reasons, living in group settings without individual attention, or frequent changes of caregivers.
- **Symptoms:** these are varied and include but are not limited to unexplained withdrawal and sadness, difficulty in social interactions, and rejection of the primary caregiver.
- RAD symptoms will develop as the child ages into either inhibited or disinhibited symptoms.
- Possible complications include self harming behavior, developmental delays, and aggression toward others.
- Diagnosis must be done by a trained professional and according to the DSM-5 diagnostic criteria.
- There are a wide range of myths around RAD and its treatment and any and all information must be explored thoroughly before application to the child.

Chapter 2:

Understanding Your Child's

Experience

Perhaps one of the most difficult things for parents or caregivers to understand about RAD is how their child feels because of the disorder. RAD causes children to present with behaviors that are very difficult to deal with and can be highly disruptive and distressing to the parent. In order to help the child heal, it is vital for parents to be able to put themselves in their child's shoes, so to speak, and understand where the behaviors are coming from.

What to Expect From a Child With RAD

Depending on how old your child is when they are diagnosed with RAD, it may be helpful to know what to expect. If your child is already a teenager, you will likely be able to spot, and finally explain, some of the behaviors that have baffled and frustrated you for so long.

Image 4: Screaming child

Behaviors from RAD children may be overt, at times, and seem aimed at pushing the caregiver away. Most often, though, these behaviors are rather subtle. Children with RAD appear to get a feeling similar to a high when they flaunt the expectations you have set or break rules. Some RAD children may go as far as physically or verbally abusing other children or pets in the home in order to push the caregiver further away. They may also reject nurturing actions in many forms including food, medication, and other necessities to life when presented by the caregiver or parent. It is not uncommon for RAD children to falsely accuse their caregivers or parents of abuse or neglect (Johnson, 2020b).

One of the most disconcerting things about RAD is that, very often, the child will behave very differently outside of the home, and therefore you may be the only one seeing the bulk of your child's RAD behaviors. People outside the home will often describe RAD children as "delightful" or "charming" when their behaviors inside the home are in stark contrast. This contrast in views can make it even more difficult for parents with RAD children to seek help because they may feel like others will not believe them if they share how the child behaves at home (Johnson, 2020b).

As we have mentioned earlier in the book, children with RAD are often more likely to display affection to strangers than their own parents. Manipulative skills are quite advanced in RAD children and they often do so in order to feel less vulnerable and more in control of what is happening around them. This manipulative behavior could include lying about the actions of their parents or caregivers in order to break down relationships (Johnson, 2020b).

Real Life Situation

I selected this story to include in this chapter as it reflects the journey that parents take when working to understand their RAD child, and how this understanding really is the key to healing. Names have been changed to protect the identity of minors involved.

People often ask Miranda and John if they feel their daughters have gotten over their Reactive Attachment Disorder. Miranda wants to say that they have, but then, at this point in their lives, she can still see damage that lingers when they are 13 and 16. Obviously the scars are still there. At least in Amanda, her 16 year old, Miranda can see that overcoming these obstacles in her life means a lot to her. Amanda is totally open to her parents helping her in situations where she needs to be socially careful. Today she is very cautious about always telling the truth, but Miranda thinks, in her heart, that she probably wouldn't trust her ability to manage when placed in a situation in which she knew she was in trouble.

Thinking back to what their family has experienced during those years after they brought the girls home from India, Miranda is reminded of the phrase, "Foresight is better than hindsight." As is the experience of many families, the whole possibility of an aversion to bonding had never occurred to them. They just automatically assumed that the child they just spent thousands of dollars to bring home to their loving arms would love them in return. Miranda admits they were really naive thinking that bringing a second child home couldn't be any harder than what they had just gone through. She jokes that they must have been gluttons for punishment. She just wishes they had been better prepared emotionally. She likes to speculate that, if she had understood what it would have taken to help Amanda and Sam, she still would have welcomed them into her home, but with a different plan of action and not wearing her heart on her sleeve.

Bitterness works against relationships, she says. As a mother who eagerly wanted to share her love and home, being rejected not just the first month, but almost the whole first five years, was more than she could bear. What Amanda needed was unconditional love, Miranda says, but repeated rejection ate away at her tender feelings, and anger and frustration replaced that love-at-first sight. Sometimes she wonders how they ever overcame it.

Image 5: Adopted child

Miranda and her husband would end up placing Sam outside of the home for five weeks after she had been with them for more than two years, with the intent to disrupt the adoption. Just having her out of the home gave them a chance to breathe again, to get their nose off the grindstone, and think about what they needed to do. Together, as husband and wife, they resolved to be Amanda and Sam's loving caregivers. In other words, the way they survived was to slip into the role that the girls needed, rather than what they as parents wanted. For a while they put aside their desire for hugs and a normal parent-child relationship. Instead, they decided to teach them to think about other people, not to laugh when someone gets hurt, not to lie, not to manipulate others, to respect their parents, and stop inappropriate destructive behavior. Still the girls' constant rejection of their mother was very difficult for Miranda.

Miranda feels like they would eventually create an environment at home that was pretty close to a bootcamp, but it was what her girls needed. She describes a typical day in her home. At 7:00 in the morning, Sam is angry and crying because she thinks someone has taken her pants. They are actually just lying on the floor near the foot of her bed. With her attitude being in this zone, it takes her an hour to get dressed, due to her cerebral palsy. This morning is no exception. When her attitude is better, she can get dressed in 10 minutes. She is not present at the breakfast table. As breakfast ends, she comes hopping into the dining room, pouting, with both legs in a single leg of her pants. Miranda sends her back to the bathroom, and removes the pants and tells her to try again. She curls up into a non-communicative ball and stares at the bathroom wall until Miranda leaves the room.

At lunch time, Sam won't eat her food without gagging. She is once again angry, yet more satisfied, realizing that everyone is upset about her antics. Pouting, she refuses to take part in the family meal and fun. After lunch, she spends time on the toilet before nap time, she is very smelly. At 5 years old, she is in the habit of letting small amounts of poop out all day, as the urge takes her. Getting into the bath is another difficult scene as she hates to take cold baths, but that is the treatment for letting poop out all day and pasting it on the wall, herself and toys. Later, with a scrub brush and bucket of soapy water, she cleans the items she smeared with poop earlier when she thought no one was looking.

After her nap comes music time. Sam enjoys listening to a certain collection of songs. The others would like a change after an hour of the same songs. Sam gets angry and pinches her brother. Miranda comes into the room to settle the disturbance and smells poop again. Off to the bathroom for another cold bath.

Dinner time presents a very hungry Sam. She eats very quickly. She knows that ice cream is coming for dessert. This time there is no gagging and no complaining. She starts pouting because she is not served ice cream first. Miranda makes sure she is last, due to demanding to be first.

Bedtime is another scene. Physical affection is another form of torture for her. She hates hugs and willingly goes to bed early to avoid them. She hides under five blankets—she took some off her sister's bed—and poops a little again.

Today, when Miranda reads this scene described in her journal, she can hardly believe that the little Sam she described is the same one that now comes to her each night and asks for a bedtime blessing and a hug. What is more amazing to Miranda, though, is what has transpired in her own heart. As damaged as her girls were and as inadequate as she felt to help them, through consistency and putting their own feelings aside to give the girls what they needed, her and her husband have truly turned their lives around.

If she had known that getting off the plane in Seattle, Washington, with her new daughter Amanda, age 21 months, would lead to five years of struggles, pain and rejection from her, she might have armed herself with more resolve. At first, she trusted her hope that within six months or so, she would stop behaving negatively. Instead it only got worse. Amanda tried to pit Miranda and her husband up against each other. She loved and obeyed her father, but hated her mother. Her primary caregiver was the enemy. Amanda loved men in general and somehow, even at an early age, was able to wrap them around her finger emotionally.

On occasions, Miranda recalls the behaviors being terribly comical. Like the time one of the girls took one little bite out of every apple in a whole big box and then threw them all over the floor. After all, she remembered thinking, how much damage can a tiny-for-her-age, 5-year-old blind girl do? The steady diet of rejection, though, had ripped a huge hole in Miranda's heart. As a woman who strove to be a good example to her children in how to be obedient to authority, love her family, and serve them with joy, all she could see was her increasing failure. She felt totally sabotaged. What had begun as an act of love for Amanda, Sam, and her family, had turned into a pile of "dirty rags", as she describes it. When the family was at the worst point in their relationship, each morning Miranda would groan with dread, as she got showered and dressed. She had to be in the same room with Amanda while she worked hard to make Miranda crumble and, to her it felt, that she was working to prove that her love was not good enough for her.

One morning, after a round of morning sickness, tears, prayer, and talking with her husband, he gently told her that she did not need to love Sam herself. She needed to let her actions show her love in the way that Sam needed. Miranda sat back on her pillow and mused for a moment. Suddenly, she says, it was as if all the bitterness that had accumulated over the last few years drained out her big toe. She knew that she loved Sam, but she didn't need to show it in the way that she wanted to, she needed to show it in the way Sam was able to receive it. Miranda thought that she could handle that. In other words, she stopped taking Sam and Amanda's damaging behavior personally. In fact, in viewing herself as a caregiver, she felt totally released to be the loving mother that she needed to be. Their rejection, misbehavior, and hateful ways were nothing but a result of what had happened to them before they came into her home. Miranda acknowledged that it was her job to help them reach a point of healing. Allowing the emotional sickness in their hearts to affect her personally rendered her unable to help them. Just like a doctor that catches the illness of his patient makes him useless as a physician to help his patient get well.

Miranda says she now understands that each child affected by early emotional damage and bonding issues tries to disprove the love of his new family to avoid further hurt in his heart. Letting another take authority in their lives is scary. They cannot let go and let someone else be in charge of them for long. Self-preservation is a powerful drive, and, once again, trust is an issue. Miranda does not believe that there is one therapy that fits all to help children or adults with RAD heal. She thinks that no matter what a family implements as treatment, be it trained counselors, reading therapy, or a boot camp like environment, the most important aspect in healing is time, coupled with consistent love in a way that the child is able to receive it.

Miranda acknowledges not all families are suited to raise children with RAD. Tough love is not for everyone. You need to be tougher than a brick, she says, mean as a she-bear with cubs, and harder than a steel ball to crack. Although there may not be a lot of parents out there like this, Miranda says that she knows a lot of families that have had no choice but to become like this to survive. For them, their relationship as husband, wife, and child meant more than personal comfort. These families are survivors in her opinion. Occasionally, she has come across parents who adopt children with RAD just for the sheer enjoyment of the challenge. As unbelievable as it sounds they are doing an excellent job and have several RAD children at one time in the home! What do they have that makes them capable of parenting children who are emotionally damaged? Thick skin. They are not easily offended, not easily hurt, and have an understanding that damaged children are just that. Damaged children.

Today, Miranda is appreciative of Amanda's hard work in helping her around the house. She now loves to please her mother and father and craves approval and love. This is totally normal for children who have come out of RAD and are trusting parental authority. She describes Amanda as a wonderful treasure. She says that Sam still has a ways to go, but her other handicaps make it more of a challenge.

Miranda says that she just wants to provide encouragement to those who are hurting right now while they deal with their RAD children. Rejection, mistrust, anger, daily horrible misbehavior, the child seeking to pit one parent against the other and then quickly turning on the charm for strangers while they hate their parents are all awful things to live with. She asks such parents to keep in mind that bitterness is truly the enemy, not their children. Making it through one day without a melt down emotionally is truly a triumph. She recommends depending on your faith or internal strength to make it through the incredible anger a child might display when asked to do a simple command or when committing an even more heinous offence. That, she says, is the only way to survive.

She advises making an extra effort to talk calmly and kindly with one another as husband and wife as a child seeks to destroy your marriage over a piece of candy. If you cannot leave your child with a sitter to get some alone time with each other because of lying, manipulation, or misbehavior, set a time to have a quiet dinner at home. Put the children in another room or in bed if they cannot behave. It surely won't hurt them to read a book (or scream alone) for an hour or two. Above all, make it plain that you are going to have a good time in life, with or without them behaving.

Miranda sometimes struggles with wondering whether she is a maid or a mother? She is grateful that she has developed the ability to feel like being both, even to her two girls, who at first did not want the mother part (Christian Homes and Special Kids, n.d.).

I think that Miranda's story provides a phenomenal lesson to all RAD parents. Often, the biggest struggle is wanting to simply be a loving parent to a child that does not want that. Miranda was able to reach a point of acceptance where she understood that, at that point in their lives, her daughters did not need a mother, they needed a caregiver that would care for their physical and emotional needs in the way that a child with RAD needs. Eventually, by accepting this and being willing to act in this role, she was able to become the mother that she wanted to be, and this is the deal that most parents of RAD children need to make. There is no need to add an element to the struggle by chiding yourself for not being able to give your child the affection and love that you think they need. In time, if you are able to meet their true needs as a RAD child, you will be able to do that, but there will be a significant period of time in which that will not be your role. Accepting that will make your life and that of your RAD child much easier.

Understanding Your RAD Child

One of the most important things to understand about a child living with this disorder is that, due to the circumstances they experienced, they have been unable to form trust bonds with others. It is vital to accept that any abuse, neglect, or traumatic experience they suffered before the age of five still affects them deeply. Due to the development of RAD in these children, certain milestones have been missed, specifically with regard to emotional development. This means that they often do not have the maturity to think any further than themselves and their own desires and needs. They essentially often behave at the emotional level of a two-year-old: focusing solely on what they can get from others, on how their own needs can be met, and what is happening in the moment without a thought for consequences. Just a toddler may throw tantrums if they don't get what they want, so will children and teenagers with RAD. While this could be seen as them simply acting out, it is important to understand that this is the only way a RAD child knows to resolve a situation.

Children living with RAD are in a constant state of survival and vigilance, much like sufferers of PTSD. These children have learned that they can only rely on themselves and go through their lives with this in mind, constantly on the lookout for situations in which they may need to protect themselves, at least in their view.

Experiences that non-RAD people may find enjoyable, such as close family relationships, expressions of love, and efforts at nurturing, are difficult for RAD children to deal with as they have come to see these as negative. As hard as it is for parents and caregivers to accept, the care and love they wish to express toward their RAD child is experienced by them as threatening and suffocating, and in order to understand their reactions, this must be accepted. The completely normal appearance of RAD children belies the battles that rage within them on a daily basis and it is our job as parents and caregivers to these children to do our best to comprehend those struggles and help the child to heal (Del Luca, 2013).

Chapter Takeaways

- RAD children purposely break rules in order to push away the caregiver.
- Aggression may be aimed at parents, siblings, or pets.
- Some RAD children will turn their repelling behaviors inward and self harm.
- The behavior outside of the home will usually be completely different from inside the home.
- It is vital to make the effort to understand your RAD child as much as possible.
- Your child's behaviors are as a result of their disorder.

Chapter 3:

Laying the Foundation in Your

Home

When my son was eventually diagnosed, and I started to understand the disorder better, I realized that my home and our parenting style centered around surviving my child's outbursts. We were living in survival mode as much as Craig was, and this was, perhaps, one of the most difficult parts of our healing process. My husband and I had to relearn how to parent our child with his diagnosis in mind.

Regardless of how RAD developed in your child, in order to promote healing, parents and caregivers need to lay a foundation in the home for improvement in behavior from the child. Consistency and understanding are key. You are not going to be able to discipline RAD out of your child, in fact, that will only make it worse. There are many ways that the home environment can be structured to facilitate healing.

Providing a Healing Environment for RAD Children

A child living with RAD needs to be a safe environment where their physical and emotional needs are consistently met. This is often what was missing from the child's life to cause the disorder and providing it is key to recovery. The primary role of a parent or caregiver in the healing process of a child with RAD is to provide safety. This is the starting point of all healing for a RAD child.

Image 6: Scared child

The RAD child needs a stable and nurturing environment in order to heal. They need tight boundaries, firm structure, and constant supervision. The RAD child will do best when they are given a range of choices to make themselves along with limits imposed by their caregivers.

It is important to remember that, for a child with a behavioral disorder, safety is not what most of us imagine. When non-RAD people think about a comforting, nurturing and safe environment they will likely picture plenty of verbal and physical affection, hugs, kisses, and caring words. For RAD children, these displays trigger their fear response, making them feel uncomfortable and threatened. This is difficult for non-disordered people to comprehend as it is so profoundly counterintuitive to us. A far better approach for a child with RAD is to acknowledge that they are hurt or struggling, help the child to identify what it is that they need to feel better, and help them to get what they need. This means that you have to hold back your natural instinct to apply what you believe is the correct fix and instead allow the child to tell you the solution. In the beginning, this will be difficult, not just because you are overriding your natural urge to nurture, but also because the child may initially find it difficult to express their needs. With persistence and consistent application, the child will learn to become more self aware and identify exactly what their needs are (Smarter Parenting, n.d.).

Although RAD children commonly push back against structure, it is important to have a strictly regimented routine and boundaries within your home. While a non-disordered child may benefit from time to themselves, a child with RAD will use this time to create chaos. This means a far greater time commitment and attention from the parent or caregiver, but it is necessary to promote healing and avoid negative behaviors. By having a closely followed routine, the parent will also have the opportunity to better monitor the child's behaviors and the symptoms they display. This can help to identify patterns in behavior and triggers which is an important part of treatment (Smarter Parenting, n.d.).

As much as structure is important, it is equally important not to share your routine plans with your RAD child. Sharing the routine gives them space and opportunity to sabotage the plans. It is fine to share the details of your planned routine with your non RAD children, although care should be taken to ensure that this is not done in such a way to isolate the RAD child and reinforce their view that they are not part of the family structure. Ideally, you want all family members to be on board with the healing process so that interaction with the RAD child is consistent and supportive in the correct way. Responsibility for helping your child to heal remains yours. It is important that any non-disordered children in the household do not feel like their lives revolve around helping their sibling to heal (Smarter Parenting, n.d.).

A RAD child feels constantly insecure. A vital part of their healing is to find ways to increase their sense of security. This can be accomplished by establishing clear expectations for behavior so there is no question as to what is and isn't acceptable. Response to any violation of these expectations must also be consistent and predictable. RAD children will do their best to push your buttons, but they are not doing it from a place of spite, their disorder simply does not allow them to behave otherwise until their feelings of insecurity and the other symptoms of RAD are slowly dealt with. The implementation of loving and consistent boundaries makes the world a less frightening place for your RAD child. When they are able to consistently predict how you will react to certain behaviors, they are far less likely to constantly try to push the limits to repel you (Johnson, 2020b).

When your child is presenting with difficult behaviors or feeling upset, it is important to stay calm but do take charge. Ignoring the behaviors will not help just as lashing out in frustration will not help either. If you ignore the behavior the child will continue to present with increasingly frustrating behavior to achieve the reaction they seek. If you lash out, you essentially rewarded the disordered instinct. When reacting to the behaviors of RAD children, understand that their negative behavior is an external sign that they do not know how to handle what they are feeling and need your assistance. Although it can be difficult, it is necessary to ensure that you do not take your child's behavior personally. It is not a reflection of your parenting or you as a person, and it is important to keep that in mind. By remaining calm, you provide your child with the assurance that what they are feeling can be handled without having a meltdown or negative behavior. Your reaction to their behavior will set the stage for their own healing (Johnson, 2020b).

As difficult as it may be to immediately reconnect with a child that is consistently displaying behavior that is aimed at annoying you, it is important to do so. By immediately reconnecting with a child that is trying to push you away, you are slowly teaching them that their efforts at distancing themselves from you are not going to work, no matter what they do. Trust will begin to develop if your child can see that you are consistently there for them in a way that doesn't overwhelm them (Johnson, 2020b).

Owning up to our mistakes as parents and adults and taking steps to initiate repair is not only for raising non-disordered children, it is important with RAD children. They need to be able to witness and trust your commitment to their healing. By understanding that you are willing to own up to your imperfections, RAD children will come to understand that they will be loved no matter what.

Every family goes through periods of change, whether it be a relocation, job change for a parent, or addition of a new sibling. RAD children are especially sensitive to change, and, during these times, it is even more important to ensure that you are maintaining a predictable and safe routine to avoid regression (Nicole, n.d.).

Making a RAD child feel loved takes a very different form than the same act in non-RAD children. As we have already discovered, the same tactics that elicit a feeling of being loved in most people often have an opposite effect on those with RAD. If a child has not bonded with a caregiver early in life, they will often find it difficult to accept physical displays of love, but with time and patience you can teach them to accept such displays. The key here is to identify actions that do feel good to your child and that they are able to accept as displays of affections. Examples of this could include, cuddling, rocking, or hand holding. These may represent attachment experiences that the child missed out on in early life. Where the child has experienced significant physical abuse in the past, this process will need to be approached very carefully and slowly as the child may be highly resistant to physical contact.

With RAD children, we are often dealing with an individual that is at a lower emotional age than their physical age and it is important for parents to consider this during interactions. It is not possible or fair to compare your RAD child to another in its age group or your own older non-RAD child at that age. This may mean that more nonverbal communication is required to soothe and comfort (Nicole, n.d.).

RAD children need significant assistance in processing and expressing their emotions so that they do not do so in a negative way. As a parent or caregiver, you will need to reinforce the notion that all feelings are okay to experience and help them find healthy ways to understand and express all of their emotions.

It is vital to carve out periods of time in your schedule where you focus all of your attention solely on your RAD child. This time can be used simply to listen to them, to have a conversation about what is happening with them, or to play a game they enjoy. This helps the child to feel that your full, focused attention is on them, but in a way that they enjoy and does not feel threatening to their RAD instincts.

In conversing with your child, come up with affirmation statements of commitment and love. Try to immerse yourself in these statements so that they become second nature as you will need to use them in the most heated of situations and when your child has exhibited some of the most difficult behaviors to accept. Such affirmation statements could include, "Even though you lashed out at me earlier and called me names, I love you, and will be here for you no matter what." Statements like these provide a sense of security for RAD children as they understand that no matter what they do, they cannot drive you away (Nicole, n.d.).

Caring for the physical health of RAD children is just as important as caring for their emotional health. Healthy lifestyle habits can go a long way to helping to reduce your child's levels of stress and levelling out any mood swings. When RAD children are well rested, relaxed, and feel physically well, it is much easier for them to manage emotional challenges.

From a diet perspective, you definitely want to cut out processed sugars as much as possible and be sure to include lots of whole grains, vegetables, fruits, lots of good fats, and lean protein. Excellent sources of good fats include flax seed, fish, avocados, and olive oil. Sleep is vital to helping to maintain emotional health in all human beings and especially in children. RAD children need a consistent sleep schedule in terms of both bed time and time of waking in order to help regulate their circadian cycle (biological clock). Physical activity is very important for children that may have anger management issues. If your child doesn't naturally gravitate toward physical activity try to find sports or classes that appeal to them so that they look forward to the activity. This could be something as simple as walking dogs at a rescue center if the child is an animal lover (Smarter Parenting, n.d.) .

Real Life Situation

This real life story displays the often hit-and-miss nature of RAD in that you will hear about three biological siblings all from the same background and only one developed high-level RAD. The same interventions were applied to all three children by their parents, but only one continued to regress. It is also a story of adopted parents having to make the most difficult of decisions. Names have been changed to protect the identities of minors and their parents. It is also an example of how, unfortunately, very often when an adoption is finalized the assistance you were given as a foster parent disappears and you need to find your own way in an often difficult world.

Nadine says that it seemed to happen in an instant. From the time the caseworker called to the time the boys arrived, Nadine and Matthew had one week to prepare for parenthood. Biological brothers three-month-old Martin, 16-month-old Bryce, and three-year-old Marco, all came to their doorstep at once.

Like most new parents, Nadine and Matthew had no idea what they were doing. Still, Nadine felt mentally prepared. She always knew she wanted to adopt children. It wasn't for any particular reason, but her passion to do so was strong. In fact, it made the difference of whether she married Matthew or not. Despite him being the love of her life, she had told him that if he was not prepared to adopt children with her, she would not be able to marry him.

Matthew agreed that even if he and Nadine decided to have biological children, they would adopt as well. A year later, they became foster parents with the intent to adopt three sons.

Nadine and Matthew were overwhelmed with three young children, as anyone can imagine. The biggest struggle, though, was with Bryce.

He would scrunch up his face, fists balled, and scream for hours on end, day after day. The more Nadine and Matthew tried to soothe him, the louder and more upset he became. Although Nadine understood how early trauma impacted the brain, she and Matthew did not understand the severity of it. They had no idea that Bryce was actually struggling with Reactive Attachment Disorder—the result of early childhood trauma that changes the brain and inhibits trust and authentic relationships.

Nadine and Matthew felt grateful for the team of county professionals helping their family. They followed all of their advice, but as soon as they officially adopted the boys, all of the professionals and services disappeared.

Nadine and Matthew were completely on their own, still with no knowledge of RAD. No one in the county shared with Nadine and Matthew that their family could access post-adoption services. Thankfully, Martin and Marco responded well to the interventions. They still needed much more help for Bryce, though.

Bryce would sit cross-legged in his crib, just staring, not sleeping—all night long. He would pop out his window screens and run away. At age three, Bryce found a hidden pocket knife and stabbed his older brother with it. He also toppled over a high chair with his little brother sitting inside.

Although entirely capable, Bryce refused to potty train. He would urinate and defecate all over the house, primarily in the heater vents. When Bryce was six-years-old, he punched his teacher and urinated all over the principal's office. Nadine and Matthew asked for recommendations from friends, school staff, and doctors to help Bryce. Nadine quit working to meet Bryce's severe needs. They spent hundreds of thousands of dollars on multiple therapists and services. Nothing helped though, and it seemed like no one understood what was happening in their family or what to do for Bryce, including professionals. They felt hopeless.

Image 7: Mischievous child

As Bryce got older, his behaviors grew too. Nadine and Matthew felt as though they could barely deal with his disrespect, fighting, manipulation, false allegations, stealing, and lying. But his physical assaults inside their family scared them. Bryce regularly walked up to his brothers and punched them as hard as he could out of nowhere. He once slammed his older brother's hand in the door because he didn't like him standing in the doorway. He smeared his feces all over his brother's room and punched a hole through their adjoining bedroom wall. Michael and Marco grew afraid to sleep alone at night in fear of Bryce.

By age seven, Bryce had his first mental health hospitalization. The whole family was also in therapy to help them cope with living with Bryce. After his third inpatient hospital stay, all of his therapists said he needed to live in a residential treatment center for the wellbeing and safety of everyone in the family. Yet, all of the RTCs rejected his admission due to the severity of his behaviors. Bryce finally had a diagnosis of Reactive Attachment Disorder at that point, but no one knew what to do about it.

When Nadine called the county, desperate for help, they said they wouldn't do anything. So Nadine and Matthew did their best to persevere and continued to follow the advice of professionals. One day, though, Bryce's school principal called Nadine to pick him up. He had been in another fight. Upon returning home, Nadine let Bryce know his consequence for fighting—that he wasn't allowed to attend an afterschool program. As usual, he began to scream at Nadine and throw furniture all over the house.

Nadine was able to get 10-year-old Bryce to his room to contain his violent outburst. Once she got him to his room, she worked fast to remove any potential weapons she could find. When she bent down to pick up a pencil, Bryce quickly came behind her and jumped on her back.

Bryce wrapped the legs of a pair of pajama bottoms around her neck screaming obscenities, saying he was going to kill her. Nadine struggled to breathe with the tight pajamas choking her but eventually managed to get Bryce off. She got free and ran for help. Shortly after the incident, Bryce went back to the hospital. Nadine and Matthew knew he couldn't return home again this time. It was too dangerous.

After hours of research, Nadine found an online support group and learned of RAD Advocates, a nonprofit organization that supports parents of children with Reactive Attachment Disorder. They help parents in all walks of the journey, including how to secure safety for their families.

Nadine was traumatized and desperate for help the day she called RAD Advocates. As parents of children with the disorder themselves, RAD Advocates understood Nadine's situation immediately.

RAD Advocates helped Nadine prepare for the worst-case scenario that she was in. She'd need to refuse to pick Bryce up from the hospital, they said. It was the only way to demand he get the help he needed and to protect her family.

RAD Advocates talked her through the process, the documents she'd needed to gather in preparation, and a plan of action to help the whole family feel safe. They attended hospital staff and child protective services meetings to advocate for the family. In addition, RAD Advocates educated Matthew and Nadine's attorney on the disorder, and they provided additional resources that Nadine and Matthew needed to get through their court involvement. Through the help of RAD Advocates, the county took Bryce back into custody to get him the help he needed. The whole family, including Bryce, was finally safe.

Although Nadine and Matthew continue to work toward reunification, they don't foresee a time in the near future that they'll feel safe doing so. They are just now beginning to heal.

Nadine has been diagnosed with post-traumatic stress disorder. Although she still wakes up most mornings crying and hyperventilating, her nightmares, panic attacks, and insomnia are beginning to subside. Michael and Marco still share a room in fear of sleeping alone but Marco rarely wakes in the middle of the night wheezing from anxiety-induced asthma. For the first time in his life, he can sleep through most nights without a breathing treatment. And eight-year-old Michael stopped wetting the bed.

Marco, who once only grunted and followed Nadine everywhere, is now independent, comfortable in his skin, and talkative. Nadine appreciates being able to hear his thoughts, now. The boys are relaxed, happy, and living a normal childhood. They finally have friends over to the house and overnight.

Nadine says that when she dreamed about adopting children, she never imagined that the system would fail her family to the point that relinquishing parental rights was the last of her terrible options. She is grateful that NPOs like RAD Advocates exist to help without judgment when she needed to do everything she could to protect her family. She feels that they are able to understand what others aren't even able to fathom (Van Tine, 2020c).

Nadine and Matthew's story is one that forces us to realize that even laying the foundation for healing in our home is not always enough. Nadine and Matthew were able to provide the type of atmosphere that a RAD child should need to heal, but sadly for Bryce that was not enough. For someone as committed as Nadine was to adopting, realizing that after she did, she was for all intents and purposes alone, must have been terrifying. I do want to be clear that this is not always the case and there are many instances in adoption scenarios where social services provide excellent support to adoptive parents. The key really is to know what services you are entitled to and push for assistance for your family and your RAD child.

Chapter Takeaways

- The ideal environment for a RAD child is highly structured.
- Nurturing looks different to a RAD child than it does to you.
- Boundaries are imperative to healing, but at the same time be aware that initially these boundaries will be pushed against with the utmost of force.
- RAD children feel unsafe all the time, it is vital to ensure that you provide them with a secure environment.
- Your RAD child is trying to push you away with their behaviors, always do your best to respond calmly to show them that no matter what they do, their behaviors don't cause you to leave.
- Learn your RAD child's language of love and use it at every opportunity.
- Help them to care for their physical health as this is closely linked to their emotional health.

Chapter 4:

Proactive Strategies to Raising a

Child with RAD

Parenting a child with RAD is nothing like parenting a non-RAD child. Any parent that has multiple children and not all have RAD will attest to that. Strategies that work to raise a non-RAD child will often backfire horribly with disordered children and this makes parenting in a multi-child household quite a challenge. With practice, though, and good initial starting points, it does become easier. After raising my RAD son for several years before we had our second child, I can tell you that the transition was tough, but by working with our medical team, over time, it became far easier.

The key to raising a RAD child is to have proactive strategies in place. You never want to be playing catch-up with a disordered child as you will inevitably lose. It is necessary to be one step ahead at all times, and it is possible to achieve this.

How Does RAD Parenting Differ From Ordinary Parenting?

Children that experienced trauma that impacted their development are not like other children. These children have very different needs, especially if their trauma results from not having been raised by emotionally healthy adults from birth. As their needs are so different, the type of parenting strategies that work to successfully raise such a child, and help them heal, are naturally also very different.

Behavior modification strategies and tools such as rewards, chore charts and the like, might work well with non-disordered children but they do not work well with RAD children. This is predominantly because, for RAD children, it is far more important to not give up control to adults than it is to gain their approval through stickers and other forms of positive reinforcement. Unlike non-disordered children, RAD children are not motivated by gaining their parents' approval.

Family traditions, such as holidays or special occasions with gifts and decorations, can also be difficult for RAD children to deal with and it is not uncommon for them to attempt to sabotage such occasions. In their minds, this helps to emotionally distance them from their families, especially the maternal figure in the family (Nicole, n.d.).

As much as we would like to believe that love heals all, this is not the case with RAD children and, although you will be drawn to comfort them in the way that you may a non-RAD child, this will be the worst thing you can do. RAD children will only heal from a combination of professional assistance and the consistent application of the right type of parenting style (Nicole, n.d.).

Image 8: Children being affectionate

As we have already learned, affection is not welcome in RAD children. While you can find ways that are comfortable for the child to accept affection, hugs and kisses will not be enjoyed in the same way that a non-RAD child would appreciate them. Sadly, this usually only applies to the adults that are seen as the caregivers and RAD children will be openly and often inappropriately affectionate with complete strangers or acquaintances. This is not the case with all RAD children and some will reject affection from everyone. A normal reaction for a RAD child faced with an attempt at physical affection from a caregiver will be to back away or physically resist the touch by lashing out. We often see in movies that the best way to comfort a developmentally traumatized child that is lashing out is holding the child in a bear hug until they calm down. Let me be very clear, this will not work with RAD children. You will do more damage to the relationship.

RAD children need to know that you respect their boundaries. At first, they will push back, but, eventually, they will acknowledge your respect for these physical boundaries.

Negotiating is another strategy that does not work with RAD children. Their disorder makes them highly manipulative. They may even go out of their way to ensure that no negotiation is possible to see how far they can push you (Discovery Mood & Anxiety Program, 2019a).

As difficult as it is, because you know the child is not at fault for the behavior but simply the result of their disorder, it is imperative that you do not attempt to rescue your child from the consequences of their actions. Perhaps even more so than a non disordered child, RAD children need to understand that they will be held accountable for unhealthy behaviors. If they believe you will smooth things over for them all the time, they will use and manipulate you to constantly cover up for them. This is not conducive to healing and only reinforces the disordered behaviors.

Trust me, I understand from first hand experience how difficult this is. Especially if something that you, as a parent, may have done has contributed to your child's RAD. The guilt we carry causes us to want to protect our children from the consequences of the disorder. This is not helpful, and really, tough love is the only option. By forcing your child to face the results of their behavior you really are helping them, as difficult as it may be.

One of the most challenging parts of raising a RAD child is maintaining your own emotional levels. You cannot be emotionally reactive around a RAD child because this is exactly what their behaviors are trying to entice. When they see you react emotionally, they will see this as proof that they have been able to control you emotionally and they will continue to push your buttons. This is very difficult and takes a lot of practice. If there is more than one carer in the home, you will both need to be on the same page about how to react to your child's RAD behaviors. If the child sees that one parent is more emotionally reactive than another, they will not only target that parent or carer, but they may try to play the carers up against each other (Discovery Mood & Anxiety Program, 2019a).

RAD children are not thinking in logical ways and reasoning with them does not work. Their behaviors and thought patterns are disordered and your own ordered thinking does not apply to what is happening in their head. To them, your reasoning makes no sense.

The nonprofit organization, RAD Advocates, suggests documenting your child's behavior on a daily basis (2019). You may think that you will remember, but, after a week of ongoing difficulties, every behavior will meld into one in your head and the intricacies of each will be lost. The minute details about your child's behavior are extremely valuable in setting up a treatment plan for them. If you can start to see patterns, triggers, and possible solutions in context, this will help the team assisting you with your child's recovery. Documenting behavior also helps to understand which levels of medication or other treatments are working well and which need to be adjusted. Try to keep this documentation consistent even when they are not at home. So if your child has an episode at school, ask the school to keep detailed reports of this and make copies of those records to share with the mental health team. If possible, and if it is not too taxing on your child's teacher, if they are able to give you daily summaries of their behavior and triggers, that will be even more helpful. If your child is struggling so significantly that they need to be hospitalized, try to get a clear understanding of what treatments were used there and how your child responded. Safety cameras in your home can also be helpful, although you will want to be cognizant of the privacy concerns of your non RAD children and ensure that they feel comfortable in their own home. A journal is often helpful to record reactions and behaviors that may seem small and insignificant at the time, but when looked at as part of a bigger picture, will provide a good amount of information. Make notes about what was different about your child and their behavior on that day and what was the same as prior days. It will be really helpful to have a daily filing system for all of this gathered information so that it does not overwhelm you at the end of a week or month.

It is definitely important to ensure that your RAD child is as much a part of normal household routines as possible, within feasible limits. To facilitate this and also to slowly introduce expectations for their behavior and responsibilities, give the child age-appropriate tasks within the household. Do keep in mind that if the task requires any type of emotional reasoning, your RAD child is at a lower emotional level than their peers. Feel free to start with really simple tasks and work your way up to where you can see the child is still comfortable. Be aware that there is a good chance your child will initially push up against these tasks in order to get a reaction out of you so, as always, make sure they are supervised.

In parenting a RAD child, you can help them start healing in seemingly small ways that will have a major impact later. Eye contact is one such area of focus. RAD children find it extremely difficult to make eye contact, and this is definitely something you will need to work on. Learning how to make and maintain eye contact helps RAD children get a better feel for the emotions of others—something that is not usually on their radar, to their social detriment. It also helps to make the child feel more attached and connected to others. As much as you may be able to help your child develop this skill, it must be noted that when they are frustrated or distressed, this will likely fall away again, and that is not the time to press the maintenance of eye contact. Rather, start encouraging eye contact when the child is calm and when you are not in a confrontational situation. You can verbally prompt the child with a reminder to look at you. If they are not completely averse to physical contact, you could try gently touching their cheek until they look at you. Remain calm and hold off on speaking until the child is making eye contact with you. When they do, ensure that your face is pleasant and that you are smiling if the situation allows for it (Discovery Mood & Anxiety Program, 2019a).

Emotions are one of the most important things to teach your RAD child. Some RAD children can be so disconnected from their own bodies that they will struggle to identify and recognize what they are feeling. You can help them to become more self aware by letting them look at photos or looking at themselves in the mirror. Letting them see the emotions in a photo or the mirror will help them begin to associate the emotions with themselves and not an external force. Emotions sometimes have powerful physical responses in the body and while non RAD children will come to recognize how these responses match up with the emotions they are feeling, RAD children need to be taught this. You can start this by using photographs of other people expressing certain emotions. Use a photograph of a person with clenched fists and a red face to help the child link up the physical reaction that person is having with the emotion they are likely feeling is either frustration or anger. In this way, the child can start to correlate the feeling of anger, or any other feelings for that matter, with the emotion itself (Smith et. al., 2020).

As with any child, a RAD child will not understand the concept of personal choice until it is taught to them. It is vital for children to be taught how choices and outcomes are connected so that they can grasp how their choices will affect them and others. RAD children will require time and significant repetition in order to understand the true impact of even the smallest choices. You will need to be consistent about your teachings and be ready to point out each instance when it happens. Remember that you do not have to find examples of a major magnitude for the lesson to be learned. It could be as simple as a child spilling their soda on their favorite shirt because they weren't following the rules about no food or drink in the bedroom. The consequence of this may be that the soda stains and their favorite shirt is ruined. It's a small thing, but if you are looking for the lessons to teach, even seemingly insignificant events like this can be teaching experiences for RAD children. Most commonly, RAD children will take greater lessons from instances that have consequences for them personally. Once they have managed to grasp the concept, you can start to introduce the idea that their actions have consequences for others too (Smith et. al., 2020).

When approaching how their actions are connected to consequences, it may be helpful to use visual aids such as drawing, books, puzzles, and the use of whiteboards. The most vital part of this teaching process is for the child to be able to come up with their own decision and be able to link those choices to outcomes (Smith et. al., 2020).

I've covered caring for children in depth, but infants present their own challenges. Parenting RAD infants needs to be much more hands-on than with other infants. Ideally, you will want to facilitate bonding with the infant by breastfeeding, where possible, or bottle feeding with the child in a sling, facing the caregiver for at least four to six hours a day. Massaging the child with infant-specific techniques will also facilitate the child's receptiveness to physical touch. Skin to skin contact is also beneficial, as is sleeping with the parents (Del Luca, 2013).

Real Life Situation

I chose Cathy's story to share with you in this chapter because it illustrates a family with different needs and also shows how RAD can have a devastating effect on a marriage. As with previous stories, the names have been changed to protect the identities of those involved.

Cathy and her husband lived in St. Louis, Missouri with their two birth daughters when they adopted three-year-old Mika from a Russian orphanage. She says that Mika was perfect when he came, and he just blended into their family. A few years later, Cathy and her husband decided to adopt another child. During the adoption process, Cathy became pregnant and Milly was born just eight weeks after their son Henry's adoption was finalized.

Henry and Milly entered the picture when Mika was seven and, after no previous signs, his behavior took a turn for the worse. Cathy talked about the transition saying that before, he was in control, he was the little prince with his two princesses. All of the sudden, cute little Henry came in, plus a newborn, and Mika just switched. Cathy's husband, however, could not deal with raising five children, two with behavioral issues rooted in trauma, and their marriage broke up.

Both Mika and Henry had behavioral issues that stemmed from childhood trauma. Henry had trouble physically regulating himself while Mika was quieter, deceitful, and manipulative. He would use her email account to send emails to people and also stole and hid things. Mika would also have complete meltdowns, far more severe than a normal temper tantrum. Cathy would have to secure him until he wore himself out so that he wouldn't hurt other people or himself.

Those severe meltdowns were what made Cathy come to the conclusion that she needed help; she could not do this alone. She looked for help from a therapist in St. Louis who diagnosed both children with Reactive Attachment Disorder and recommended they seek help at the Institute of Attachment and Child Development (IACD) in Colorado. Mika's behaviors, based on his early abandonment, memories of his time in the orphanage, and survival instincts now clearly manifested and escalated to extremes that even he could not comprehend. His survival instinct was in full control of him.

Mika started therapy at the IACD at ten years old. He went through the program once and returned for two weekend-long "tune-ups". Henry also went through the program, but Cathy's marriage ended in the middle, necessitating pulling him out. Cathy says that Henry didn't finish but she is not sure he could've. He didn't have the cognitive understanding to. Luckily, the best thing he had going for him was that he was not aggressive.

In addition to in-clinic therapy for Mika, clinicians also coached Cathy on remaining consistent with the things they were working on. Cathy knew that looking for help when you have acknowledged that you need it is important but following through with their coaching is also vital. She says that she truly believes that if you are seeking out help, you are trying to give them what is best for them. So, if you can't do it yourself, listen to the professionals.

Mika was not able to be a part of the family, he didn't know how and when he went to LACD, he did not want to know how. In classes for art therapy, he would sketch a picture of a boat containing his family and he was drawn in the water surrounded by sharks. That is how he felt but that is also where he would rather be: encircled by sharks rather than with his family.

At times, Cathy says, following the advice she was given at the Institute was difficult, and the separation from Mika was hard. She would ask to see the children and the therapists told her that they had to be ready to see her. They had to choose her to be their mom. Mika used to say, "I didn't pick you as my mom, you picked me. I was happy in an orphanage. I had all my friends there." Cathy understands that he simply did not know any different. The therapists taught her how to be firm, provide consistency, and follow through on expected consequences. She became a tough mom because that's what they needed.

Having children with RAD was alienating. Mika behaved normally around friends and family, but when he was at home he was a different child. He was so good at masking his behavior that no one outside of the home believed her. People thought she was lying, crazy, or wrote it off as boys just being boys. No one else thought he needed therapy.

When Cathy became the tough mom that Mika needed, people thought she was being too harsh with her children. They did not understand. They did not see the behavior Mika presented with at home. They would say things like, "Did you hear she took all the stuff out of his bedroom and made him sleep on just a mattress? Why would she adopt someone that she's going to treat like that." These people simply did not understand what was going on inside the family unit.

When Cathy met her current husband, he found it difficult to grasp the concept of RAD; a child unable to attach or love seemed so strange. It took her new husband less than a year to realize what Reactive Attachment Disorder did to a child. He once said, "You can clearly see that after about 30 minutes in a room with you, Henry starts to get uncomfortable with you. Not anyone else. It's almost like he starts to get allergic to you and pushes you away."

Cathy points out the importance of support. She started a support group in St. Louis for parents of RAD children and she still connects with these parents today. They all understand each other and most valuable of all, there is no judgment.

Cathy suggests that to find support, parents must first seek out a doctor for diagnosis. That will, in turn, will lead you to therapists and resources to help.

She warns parents that there are not very many organizations that really understand RAD and some will try treatments like cognitive therapy that will often just send a RAD child in circles. In St. Louis, resources were scarce, and this is why she went to Colorado for help. She says that she has been out of this for almost two decades and, back then, there were three people in her area that were really working on attachment disorders. They are still the only ones and two of them have retired. The resources just don't exist in the Midwest, she says.

When asked if she could tell the therapy was working, Cathy told two different stories about Henry's progress. Henry was fascinated by people in uniform. On the flight out to Colorado, he went up to the cockpit to receive the wings he had seen other kids receive. He came back with an angry co-pilot who told her that he started off the same way as every other curious child asking about the various switches and buttons, but then he had asked which lever would smash the plane into the buildings like what happened on 9-11.

After he completed the therapy, they had been in a restaurant, and, again, he was drawn to pilots, this time a table of them. While Cathy was hesitant about what he would say to them, she allowed him to talk to them. When he came back, she asked what he talked to them about. "One of them was a girl. I've never seen a girl pilot," he said in response. He had just had a normal conversation with them without inappropriate and unexpected comments.

With Mika, Cathy noticed that he was different when she could see him socially interacting with other people and he wasn't displaying any manipulative behavior. He was just behaving as any normal boy would. She says that her children are known to be responsible, respectful, and a joy to be around. Cathy says that when they started to do that, she knew they were getting better.

Today, Cathy's three oldest children are all out of college. Henry still lives with disabilities that prevent him from leading an independent life including fetal alcohol syndrome and Reactive Attachment Disorder. While the medication and therapy would work for a while, things wouldn't always be permanent. Henry is now in the Easterseals program and requires 24 hour care.

Mika has come full circle. After getting his BSC degree in sociology, he found a job as a clinical aide helping children just like him. Cathy and Mika now have a close relationship. After the program at the IACD, he learned how to be a part of the family and he was able to choose her to be his mom (Institute for Attachment and Child Development, n.d.).

There are two parts of this fascinating story that I wanted to point out because they illustrate the mind of a RAD child. The first is Mika's statement that he didn't choose Cathy to be his mother and that he was quite happy in the orphanage with his friends. This, of course, is a devastating thing for any parent to hear, but it also highlights the fact that Mika, as a RAD child, had no way of valuing the family unit or a mother figure. His survival instincts told him that he did not need nurturing and, in fact, that nurturing was bad and dangerous. If Mika did not have RAD, he would have been able to fully grasp how lucky he was to have the opportunity to live life in a family unit. Thankfully, through healing and help, he was eventually able to grasp that.

The other interesting aspect of this story is the drawing that Mika did in art therapy. By representing himself in the water with the sharks while his family was safely in the boat, without consciously knowing it, he drew a perfect representation of RAD. RAD forced Mika to stay in the water with the sharks by convincing him it was the best place to be. Even though, at any time, he could reach out and be pulled to safety by his family in the boat, his RAD convinced him that staying in the water was the far better option. This is not something that we can reason out of children with RAD. You will never be able to explain to them how skewed this thinking is because it is the nature of the disorder.

Communicating Effectively with a RAD Child

Effective communication with a RAD child is crucial and needs to be undertaken in a different way. Learning how to communicate effectively with your RAD child can improve your relationship and aid in the treatment process. When you make an effort to communicate with your child in a way that meets their needs, they also come to understand that you are working hard to help them with their challenges. This will help foster trust between you as the parent and the child.

There are some steps you should follow that will help you to develop effective communication skills with a RAD child:

Step 1: Look at the child. Remember we are trying to teach the child that eye contact is good and when we communicate with others, we show them that we are doing so by looking at them.

Step 2: Use their words. It will not be helpful if your child does not understand the words or terminology you are using. Speak to them using the vocabulary level they use and try to use any specific terms they may have developed for their challenges. This also means carefully understanding what they are saying when they talk. You could start a conversation off, for instance, by saying, "When you said that you wanted to hurt me, what were you feeling just then?"

Step 3: Clarify. This connects to the previous step. Never assume that you understand what is going through the mind of a RAD child. Always make sure that you clarify their meaning and the intention behind their statement and action. The dots that you join in your mind, with your ordered thinking, may not be the same picture that is in the mind of the RAD child.

Step 4: Reflect back what they understood. Once you have been able to clarify what the child was thinking at the time, reflect this back to them to give them an opportunity to hear it come from you. This often helps to provide a different perspective. You could try saying something like, "So when you said that you wanted to hurt me, you were actually feeling some anger because I maybe didn't listen to the way you wanted me to, and that was where the anger came from?" As I've mentioned before, it's important for your child to see that you are willing to admit to and take responsibility for your mistakes. If in trying to understand your child's feelings or actions, you discover that you may have inadvertently contributed, acknowledge that and try to do better next time. Even if you have played a role in the development of the behavior, though, that does not take away the RAD child's responsibility for their reaction. They still need to understand that telling someone they want to hurt them is not a healthy way to respond if a person is not listening to you well enough.

Step 5: Come to an understanding. This can be a tough one because RAD children are not great negotiators. They are often not willing to budge from their standpoint and this can make coming to an understanding difficult. Your child may not agree to what you are saying, but successful communication is not always tied to agreement. Rather it is more important that both parties understand the other's viewpoint. Explain how you feel when your child tells you they want to hurt you (in this example) and ask them if they can understand that you feel that way. Remember, they don't need to agree that you feel that way, they just have to understand what you are saying. Coming to an understanding may mean different things in different contexts, and sometimes it's not worth forcing the issue. As long as you feel that the child has been able to express themselves in a healthy way and that some level of resolution has been reached, feel free to take a step back (Smarter Parenting, n.d.).

In order to get the most out of this systematic communication tool, try to use it daily and in as many situations as possible. It is most important for RAD children to focus on repeating and clarifying what is being said. It is easy to misunderstand a disordered child's communication and do more harm than good. As much as possible, try not to counsel or correct the child during the discussion. You want to encourage free and open communication and you don't want the child to feel that you are judging them for their thoughts. This open course of communication will help to build trust between you and the child. The child will feel that they can express what they really feel without judgment as long they are open to discussion.

You can address any concerns that you have about matters that have arisen in the discussion at another time. During this conversation, you can use the same five-step procedure and allow your child to explore and examine your perspective by reflecting back and clarifying what was heard.

Preventative Teaching for RAD Children

A large part of parenting a RAD child is putting preventative measures in place to avoid the behaviors you don't want and encourage the behaviors you do want. Because ordinary methods of behavior correction do not work with RAD children, it is necessary for us, as caregivers, to get into the habit of encouraging alternative behaviors before the negative behaviors are displayed. This will help the child understand that they have an option to behave differently and they do not need to be controlled by their disorder.

This can be undertaken through a five-step procedure as follows:

Step one: Start with positive empathy. This is a fine balance with RAD children because, although you want them to know that you understand that their behaviors are emanating from their disorder, you do not want them to think that it is okay to use their disorder as an excuse. Displaying positive empathy for their actions or position on something means doing your best not to stigmatize the child as being "bad" for behaving in a way that is considered negative or unhealthy. Really, you want the child to understand, through this process, that although the disorder they live with is causing them to behave this way, they can still take responsibility for choosing to behave in a different way.

Step two: Describe what you want. At this stage of the process, you are providing your child with another, more acceptable option for their behavior. While these other options may seem obvious to a person with ordered thinking, a RAD child may not be able to formulate these options for alternate behavior on their own, and it is our job to teach them what their alternatives are. Try to be as clear as possible when describing the behavior you would like to see and ensure that the child fully understands what you mean and how they can act out that behavior.

Step three: Give a meaningful reason. Even more so than most children, RAD children are unlikely to accept an instruction at face value, and they will need a very meaningful reason for your request to really take it seriously. Consider what a meaningful reason may be to your child. Keep in mind this reason will need to contain elements of how it affects them personally, especially if they have not yet come to deeply care about the wants and needs of others. Do also combine aspects of how the behavior affects others as this will start to reinforce that link between cause (decision) and effect (outcome).

Step four: Practice expected behavior. For any child, acting something out is a valuable way to learn and will help considerably to instill the alternative behavior choice in their minds. If you like, you can act out the behavior yourself first and then ask the child to join in. You can swap roles and act out the preferred behavior as many times as you need to for it to really start to sink in.

Step five: Find a positive. Self image can be problematic for RAD children so it is quite vital to find as many opportunities as possible to praise them. While you are going through this process, keep an eye out for anything they are doing really well or behaviors that are positive and tell the child how well they are doing. Even just a willingness to participate in the process is worthy of praise (Smarter Parenting, n.d.).

Continue to practice steps one through four as often as possible until you start to see the expected behaviors becoming automatic for the child.

Image 9: Practicing good behaviors

The notes that you have started to make about your child's behavior will be imperative here as you can begin to pick up patterns of behavior and triggers that precede certain actions by the child. You can use this system to practice alternative behaviors in response to the situations that you have determined trigger your child. In this way, you are practicing preventative measures to avoid the behaviors you don't want.

Be sure to practice the alternative behaviors at least three times. Unplanned practices can also be beneficial. For instance, after the first practice, let them know that you will be practicing again later that day to see if they can remember what to do. Do this on several occasions over the next few days. This unplanned practice helps the child to start integrating the behavior into their natural response to the determined triggers. Be sure to reward the child if they do well during practice (Smarter Parenting, n.d.).

How to Effectively Praise a RAD Child

Children with RAD can have a difficult time receiving and accepting compliments and praise. Their thought patterns are not set up to acknowledge your approval so it will take time for them to accept it as a good thing. It is important to teach your child how to accept praise and compliments in an appropriate way. Teach them that it is okay to simply say "thank you," when they receive praise and it is not acceptable to reject or argue with the compliment. Even if they find the praise difficult to accept at that moment, the child needs to understand that the person offering it is doing so sincerely, and they can accept that person's point of view and mull over it later without aggressively refuting it.

Sincerity in praising or complimenting, of course, is key. RAD children are really good at detecting insincerity and, if they detect this from you, it will damage your trust relationship (Smarter Parenting, n.d.).

Well-structured praise for a RAD child will include a description of the positive behavior followed by a brief reason describing why the behavior is positive and a reason that they should repeat the behavior in the future (Smarter Parenting, n.d.).

Chapter Takeaways

- Parenting a RAD child is immensely different from parenting an ordered child, at least in the beginning while they are healing.
- Ordinary parenting techniques do not work with RAD children.
- Documenting your child's behavior on a regular basis is vital to aiding long term care and recovery.

- RAD children are often developmentally delayed and cannot be expected to behave in the same way as an ordered child.
- You will need to consciously teach your RAD child about things that other children may easily pick up on their own. This includes eye contact, identifying emotions, and the link between choices and consequences.
- You will need to communicate with your RAD child in very specific ways to get through to them.
- With RAD children, prevention of negative behavior is key.
- The method of praise that you use for ordered children will not be accepted by RAD children. You will need to teach your child to accept praise.

Chapter 5:

Handling Bad Behavior

Parenting a child with RAD can feel like being a firefighter, constantly trying to put out the fires of their negative behaviors. By using some of the preventative measures we discussed in the previous chapter, we can avoid many instances of negative behavior and start to give the child options for doing things differently. This helps significantly, but the healing process will inevitably involve some negative and difficult behaviors. It is important to know how to deal with that in the moment.

Dealing with negative behaviors in the incorrect way can actually damage the healing process and cause regression in the child. Knowing what to do when things go wrong is vital (Nicole, n.d.).

Giving Consequences

In the previous chapter, we discussed the importance of teaching your child how their decisions are connected to outcomes or consequences, both for them and for others. By ensuring that the consequences for their actions are consistent and reasonable you will provide the child with a sense of certainty. An increased level of certainty for a RAD child decreases their levels of fear and anxiety.

The nature of the RAD child's disorder means that they are constantly trying to push boundaries to see what will repel you. If they receive inconsistent reactions for the same behavior, this will increase the desire to continue pushing. Continued inconsistent reactions teach them there is a good chance they can achieve their disordered goal of pushing you away (Nicole, n.d.).

Consequences will not necessarily be helpful in preventing future behaviors, but they do provide the child with an environment that is low in fear and anxiety, meaning they will be less likely to act out in future. While an ordered child is capable of quite quickly forming an association between good consequences and certain action, RAD children take a little longer to form those connections. Even though the child may well know right from wrong, this may not necessarily mean that they will behave any differently, but they will be able to grasp the concept. Consequences will help them understand what to expect from the outside world.

Image 10: Consequences

It may be tempting to rescue your child from the consequences of their actions, but it certainly is not healthy. The period that a child spends in the care of a healthy adult is intended to prepare them for later life. They will begin to recognize that actions have consequences. If you take away the consequences, the learning loop is broken, and they will have no idea how to deal with failure in later life.

Effective Consequences for RAD Children

Due to the disordered nature of the RAD child's thought patterns, they may view consequences differently than an ordered child. It is important that you understand which consequences will be effective in impacting your child. Very often, a RAD child will exploit predictable consequences. This will especially happen if they feel that the excitement of behaving negatively outweighs the consequence you have set for that action. When misbehaving is more valuable to them than being complacent, of course they will choose to misbehave (Renee, n.d.).

As we know, RAD children are geared to push their parents and caregivers away. They reject closeness with the caregiver and do not want to be controlled by their presence. It is for this reason that the "time-out" method of behavior correction that works so well for ordered children, has the opposite effect on RAD children. By giving a RAD child a time-out, you are giving them exactly what they want—distance from you. Instead, I recommend practicing the opposite technique: a "time-in.". This means that the consequence for their action is that they do not get time away from you and instead must be by your side everywhere you go. This works particularly well with RAD children because they are essentially getting the exact opposite of what they wanted. There are certainly exceptions to this technique; if the child is being particularly aggressive or violent, it may not be the best time to practice a "time-in." If you feel like you actually need some distance from the child at that moment, it is also more than acceptable not to practice this method (Renee, n.d.).

Restitution is another technique that works well with RAD children. Here, they are expected to show that they are remorseful for their behavior by using actions rather than just words. It can become very easy for a manipulative RAD child to pick up on the fact that if they apologize everything goes away, and they may use this to their advantage. That is why it is vital to change this up as often as possible and have the child find ways to actually prove their remorse. An example of this could be having the child give up their pocket money to pay for a sibling's toy they broke in anger. This consequence is tangible and is something that even young children can take on board (Renee, n.d.).

As we know, many negative emotions have a physical component and burning off energy can help to reduce the intensity of the emotion. Anger and frustration can be aided by engaging the child in a physical activity such as running or swimming.

Distraction and redirection is a technique that usually only works with very young ordered children, but it works well beyond the toddler period with RAD children because they are often developmentally delayed. When the child is in the crux of a meltdown, it is often helpful to take them out of the setting that they are in and introduce a setting they find pleasant and relaxing. You can also switch their mindset by introducing a favorite activity that they enjoy. Once their emotions have started to subside, you can introduce a conversation about what happened earlier. By introducing a pleasant setting or favorite activity you can help to break down your child's defense mechanisms and allow for a free and honest conversation and helps to improve your access to your child's feelings and thoughts.

Do not give consequences to your child that interfere with your own mood or plans. If you do this you will feed into your child's desire to influence you and push you away. The child should never feel that their negative behavior is resulting in major changes in the household as this is exactly what their disordered thinking seeks.

Tips for Correcting Behavior in RAD Children

When correcting unwanted behaviors in RAD children, ensure you use gentle communication or non-verbal language. You must also ensure that your body language is congruent with what you are saying. RAD children are highly sensitive to non-verbal cues, and if your body language does not match up with what you are saying, they will not feel like they can trust you (Renee, n.d.).

RAD children will not always understand what they have done wrong as they are only following their instincts. The first step in behavior correction is to be sure that the child really understands why their behavior was not acceptable. This is also where our alternative behaviors come in as, once they understand what they have done wrong, they will need to know how they should behave instead. Once they understand how they should behave, you should also provide them with an understanding of the consequences of acting out the unwanted behavior, and give them the opportunity to practice the desired behavior several times.

Set Clear Boundaries for Yourself

You will often find yourself in highly emotionally charged, desperate situations when trying to stop your child's negative behavior. We are parents and caregivers to very special and unique children, but we are also human beings and everyone has a point at which they can no longer remain calm without removing themselves from the situation. It is for this reason that you need to set boundaries for yourself as much as for your child (Renee, n.d.). This needs to be done ahead of time and you will need to be really clear about what you will and won't do in specific situations where discipline is concerned. You are putting these boundaries in place to protect you and your emotional health. Even though we all enter into this journey with the best intentions, the difficulty of helping a RAD child to heal means that emotions will come up that in a discipline situation can turn into abuse without that being your intention.

Understand that you may find yourself in a situation where you are the target of violence and rage. You need to decide how to deal with violent situations when they arise. Try to have really specific plans for as many different scenarios as possible and if you focus on the worst possible scenarios, which is sometimes difficult, you will find yourself prepared for the, likely, less drastic situations.

Eliminate Battles

Do your best to eliminate battles with your RAD child as much as possible. Going into an emotional battle with a RAD child does not benefit anyone. You will be left feeling upset and the child will have achieved their goal of creating more chaos.

Rather, try to follow some of the processes I've suggested to deal with conflict, but do not get into a battle of wills with a child living with RAD.

Accuse with Confidence

When you approach your child to point out an unacceptable behavior, only do so when you are confident that you are correct in your assessment. The often manipulative nature of RAD children means that if you are not confident about your assertions, they may have you questioning your point of view. Once you feel that you are confident enough to make the assertion, ensure that you follow it up with consequences that are not going to require an enormous amount of effort on your part. As with not engaging in battles unnecessarily, you want to save your energy for situations where there is no other choice than to put your own effort into the consequences.

Rate Behaviors

You may find it beneficial to come up with a rating system for behaviors in order for a child to be able to choose the most appropriate response. Such a rating system would need to be specific to your child and each rating system will vary. Every child is different and they all present with different behaviors. Your first step should be to divide behaviors into groups by type, choose a suitable consequence for that group of behaviors, and commit both the classification and the consequence to memory. This rating system can also help to keep you focused when your child is in the grip of negative behavior patterns, as you can take some time to consider the behavior from an analytical point of view. Ask yourself what group of behaviors the pattern belongs to according to your rating system and which consequence would be applicable (Renee, n.d.).

Image 11: Rating behaviors

Such a rating system will help keep your responses consistent..

Document Everything

I know that I've said this before, but it really does bear repeating: make notes of everything and preferably on a daily, if not hourly basis. It took me some time to get into the habit of doing this and I soon realized that, for me, it was easier to use a voice recorder than write things down in the heat of the moment. I would then set aside some time at night to transcribe my voice notes for the day. Documentation like this, about behaviors, reaction to consequences, and response to different treatment methods, can become invaluable to your treatment team later on and a boon to your child's healing process (Van Tine, 2020b).

Sadly, as parents or caregivers of RAD children, we do need to be aware that the disorder is known to accompany false accusations of abuse. If this does happen, you will have detailed accounts of the child's behavior and your reaction.

What Not to Do

While so many areas with the correction of behavior in RAD children are gray and depend on the individual child, there are certainly a few things that you do not want to do. A huge one for me is never disciplining your RAD child when you are emotionally charged. Doing so has a two-fold negative effect: it makes your child feel more unsafe than they already do due to their disorder, and it actually reinforces the bad behavior because it becomes very clear that they are pushing your buttons. If you need to take a step back, keep your tone even, tell the child that you are leaving the room for a moment, and that you will return.

The second biggest thing to avoid is taking a strictly hands-off approach to disciplining a RAD child. This may well result in the child engaging in increasingly dangerous or chaotic behaviors and they may put themselves or others at physical risk. As it is so important to be consistent about consequences with RAD children, if you take a hands-off approach, you will have to do that in all situations and that is clearly unsustainable. RAD children require firm and consistent consequences so that they can establish the limits of acceptable behavior (Smith et. al., 2019).

Real Life Situation

I've included the following story as I think it illustrates the complexity and difficulty of understanding a RAD child and how, just when you think you're on top of all their behaviors, something new pops up.

In the early 90's, Emma and her husband adopted their son, Emmanuel. Diagnosed with "Reactive Attachment Disorder" (RAD) shortly after coming into their home, Emmanuel lived the life that isolated children have lived. This is the story of how they made it through those early years, the story of raising a child with RAD, and the story of their survival.

Emmanuel and his siblings had been left at a crisis in the Phoenix area by their biological mom on a number of occasions before the state took them into care. The family had been living in derelict housing and living off garbage. The State took them into care, hoping to find a family to place them all with long term. Emmanuel weighed in at just 16 pounds when he was taken into the care of the state at 16 months old.

By the time Emmanuel came to live with Emma and her husband, the boy had been placed in and removed from households where no one was related to the kids and blood family foster households. Emmanuel had been in between four and six placements. The state never did tell Emma about all of them. Four years after he was placed with Emma, he had almost doubled his body weight, hitting 36 pounds shortly after going to live with his forever family.

Emmanuel was not well cared for before moving to Emma's care. He was exposed to things no child should experience. He was not hugged often enough, he was not held often enough, and he did not receive any mental stimulation. Emmanuel survived, but he did not thrive until he was in Emma's home.

When asked what it is like living with a child that has RAD, Emma says that it is scary. It can be frustrating, and it hurts every time she thinks about what they have been through. She says that she wants to take them in her arms and make it better, but she can't. Some things are very hard to overcome. Here are the ones that were hardest for her to come to grips with:

- *Emmanuel had no differentiation between family and strangers*

- *He didn't know how to trust*
- *There was no punishment that touched him*
- *Staying connected was hard work*
- *Kids in the system lose their identity*
- *RAD kids don't have traditions*

The first day Emmanuel was brought to meet Emma and her family, he and his brother were driven to their house by their social worker, Alice. All the kids knew about them was what they had learned from Alice and from a stack of 10–15 pictures they had sent in that showed their lives.

When Alice pulled up in her car in front of their house, the two boys jumped out and headed straight towards the two of them standing on the front porch. By the time the boys got to them, they were already yelling "Hi Mom!" and "Hi, Dad!" They reached them and bear-hugged them both around their legs, professing how glad they were to meet them. After each hugging one of them, they switched parents and continued on about how much they were looking forward to being their kids. After a few moments, they both asked to see their rooms.

Now keep in mind, these boys did not know Emma and her husband. They did not even know for sure whether they were at the right house. Her husband and her talked later about how bad it would have been if Alice had stopped in front of their neighbor's place. Their neighbor was ex-military and would never have been able to handle the exuberance.

Kids with RAD often do not have any certainty about where they will be next. They treat family, friends, and strangers the same way. They either put on a brave front, pretending that they already know and adore you or they will hide from everyone for a few minutes, then decide you are lovable. RAD children do not know how to trust. They only know how to fake it.

They have been through so much trauma, they have no ability to trust anyone. They don't know how to deal with consistency. Trauma experienced at a young age damages parts of the brain that processes belief, trust, emotions, and understanding. Whether left alone because their mother couldn't care for them, shifted from house to house, or living through constant terror and pain: these kids don't know how to be real. Emma now knows that you have to teach (and sometimes reteach) them things that we consider to be the basics.

Emmanuel didn't know what the rules were at their house. He didn't know what was allowed and what wasn't, but they expected that. What they didn't expect was a kid who wanted to know the rules and the boundaries of their love, so he challenged them constantly.

Emmanuel couldn't trust there would be enough food available to him when he was hungry. He had been hungry too often in previous homes. During the night, he would sneak out of his room and into the pantry. Anything he could reach was eaten. Even if he had eaten very well during the day, he would still snack every night. Emma would find half-eaten cans of tuna in the pantry. She would find empty cans of just about anything. Any item that was sweet or full of protein would be game for Emmanuel's obsessive midnight snacking. When he could manage it, he would sneak food into his room. This was clearly to be fodder for what he believed would be hungry times in the future. It took many years for him to understand that he could eat anything in the house as long as he asked permission first.

Another item that disappeared inexplicably was toothpaste. The couple had made sure that Emmanuel knew how to brush his teeth, but for months they couldn't understand why he was going through such a huge amount of toothpaste. When they realized he had been eating it, they sat down and, once again, explained that he shouldn't eat it. They explained that toothpaste was good for brushing your teeth, but not good for eating.

Emma and her husband were technically foster parents for the first year and a bit of the placement before they finalized the adoption. During that time they learned that Emmanuel did not know how to react when he was in trouble or when things went wrong. These were two sides of the same emotional coin.

In households that he had been in previously, punishment for breaking the rules had apparently been extreme. Although Emma and her husband had never agreed with what the previous adults had done, they could. in a way, understand it. How do you punish a kid who has virtually lived independently for much of his life? What good would it do to do something like taking away dessert, especially when he had been starved? They wouldn't strike him, it wasn't good for him or for them. Any physical punishment could bring up triggering memories of prior abandonment and abuse.

Time out didn't really make any difference to him either: he would just sit for the required time, but he was just watching the clock to make them happy. He could not make the connection between the punishments and the misbehavior for a very long time.

Another side of his punishment reaction was just as difficult to deal with. Emmanuel had been hurt in the past for things that just happened. For example, he was petrified of breaking a dish or a glass. Prior foster parents had gotten mad at that and punished him harshly. The first time a glass broke when Emmanuel was around in Emma's house, he started sobbing and shaking. He knew very well that he hadn't broken the glass, Emma's husband had, but Emmanuel was completely freaked out. The first time he broke a glass, they were loading the dishwasher and he closed the door too hard. Emma's husband took him aside and told him everything would be ok. Emmanuel still looked like he had just experienced the end of the world. Emma's husband sat him down and explained to him what had happened, that it wasn't his fault, and that there would not be any punishment for him. After that Emmanuel was calmer, they opened the dishwasher and Emmanuel helped to clean up.

Emmanuel had biological siblings who did not become part of Emma's family. His sister was already living with a relative. His brother ended up staying in the system. Emmanuel didn't want to lose contact with them. Emma and her husband didn't want that to happen either. Every few months, they would reach out to the social workers to try and find his brother and arrange a visit. On each occasion it took weeks to get in touch with someone who knew where Emmanuel's brother was. The social workers were always changing. Every time the social worker was surprised that they wanted to stay in touch and that they wanted Emmanuel to know his biological siblings.

So the pattern went on and on those first years. Emma would call and find a worker who knew where Emmanuel's brother was. She would wade through the explanations time and again. Eventually when they did manage to get in touch with the right person, the contact would invariably be thrilled to find someone who knew the story of the children. The social workers were always willing to ask questions, but they weren't so willing to answer any that Emma had.

Birthdays were difficult for Emmanuel during his first few years with Emma. He wanted to see his biological siblings on his birthday, and he wanted them to come to his party. Emma and her husband tried to make this happen and Emmanuel knows they tried, but it almost never worked out.

If it was so hard just for them to keep in contact with his biological family, how much harder was it going to be for the families they are breaking up, Emma thought. Who would fight to maintain the connection? Who would fight to make sure they see or at least talk to, the ones left behind? Who would tell them the stories that they almost remember?

Kids who move around in the system don't have any records about themselves. In some states, the adoptive parents are not allowed to know anything about the child's prior placements, schooling, or health issues.

When Emmanuel went to live with Emma and her husband, he was issued with a social security number. This was not his real social security number. Emma and her husband weren't supposed to know the real one. When Emmanuel was registered for school that first year, he was registered under his prior last name. The school didn't know if they could share information with the family, as they were not yet his legal guardians. Eventually, that mess was fixed with a call from the social worker to the school.

The children did not arrive with medical records, or, not official ones anyway. They had copies of the last doctor's handwritten notes. Enough to prove to their doctor that they had been vaccinated but this was not enough for the school to agree. Emmanuel went through school "unvaccinated" because they didn't feel he should get a second dose of all the shots they had proof he had already gotten.

The kids came with one day's worth of medicine, and no prescription either. Luckily their family doctor was able to get the unofficial records and prescribe what they both took. That's also how they learned that the kids had been given a prior diagnosis of ADHD. In Emmanuel's case, that was the wrong diagnosis. Took them years to figure out what the right one was. RAD kids get lots of mental illness diagnoses beyond RAD. Whether they have other problems or not.

Emma and her husband had taken adoption certification classes when they first put their names in to adopt. Those classes were a life saver. They prepared them for most of the behaviors she's talked about. This one? It wasn't covered.

When Emmanuel came to them, he had lived through multiple family holidays—seldom with the same family more than once. He didn't know how they celebrated anything. So, he pretty much assumed they didn't celebrate. While Emma says that she has never learned what caused this reaction, she believes it is more than just the constant changes. She believes that for a kid who has been abandoned at an early age, traditions are forgotten or never learned. They just don't stick.

How do you celebrate a birthday for a child that has never received more than one present at a time? How do you celebrate Christmas? How do you teach a child that some days are special just because of the date they happen to fall on? Emma and her husband didn't know. They did their best to create their own holiday traditions, but it was difficult to stick to them. Emmanuel just didn't understand until years later what birthdays and holidays were about.

This is also one of the big fails they experienced early on. When they were told their adoption date, Emma and her husband wanted to do something special together to celebrate. To imprint the day in their memories—the day they became a family. They had a morning date with the judge, so they decided to do what any family might do: they planned a week-long trip to Disney World. They planned to surprise Emmanuel with it at breakfast before they headed to court.

Emma says that she is very glad they didn't hold the news for that morning. The week before the adoption, his teacher asked them to come to the class and talk about adoption and what it meant. As they had to schedule that, they ended up telling Emmanuel about the trip. They were leaving mid-afternoon, so they had to fit the class visit in between court and the flight. Emmanuel did not want them to come to class.

More than not wanting them to come, Emmanuel had to test the boundaries all weekend. He had to prove to himself that they wouldn't change their minds. He had started to learn that there were certain things that happened whether you were good or bad and he wanted to see how far that would reach.

Luckily, he decided before adoption day that Disney World was too big a chance to mess up. So they went. The first few days on holiday were wonderful, but then, Emmanuel hit the wall that RAD builds around children that have been traumatized early on.

In the middle of the third morning at the park, Emmanuel had a complete meltdown. Emma doesn't recall now what set it off, but it sent him into a major meltdown. Emma says that you have not seen a temper tantrum like this unless you have a RAD kid in your life. He just decided everything was wrong. Emma and her husband weren't his parents. He was going back to the judge to make him give him another family. He was going to find a payphone and call Alice to have her fly down and get him. They were mean and cruel and they didn't let him do anything. Words from the mouth of a first grader in the middle of Epcot Center just before his favorite food for lunch. They left the park, went back to their hotel room, and relaxed for a few hours. Emmanuel was still crying when they got on the bus to the hotel and still crying when they got to the room where he proceeded to fall right to sleep.

They realized that Emmanuel did not know anything about taking a vacation. He had never been on a vacation in his life. "Vacation" in his previous placements had been a trip to the cottage in Prescott for a day or two where he still had to do his chores. He didn't know how to handle everything. He convinced himself that he had to get them to send him back before they realized he needed to go back because he was damaged. "You can't love me enough. I have to push you away before you abandon me."

That event brought them full circle. Just like the first day he was with them when he hadn't known how they wanted him to act, and he hadn't known what the rules were, Emmanuel didn't know how they could possibly love him unless he was perfect. He had decided that if they weren't going to love him forever, he was going to push them away before they could realize what he really was.

Emmanuel's growing up years weren't easy on any of the family. Once he hit puberty, other problems surfaced. Those problems tore their family apart for quite a few years. There were times when they didn't know if they would see him again and at times they didn't know if he would make it to 20.

Thankfully, this story has moved into a happier chapter. Emmanuel is now 30 years old and about six foot tall. He lives with his partner and their two kids in Washington. They have their struggles as we all do, but they are a family. That's something Emma and her husband didn't know if Emmanuel would ever have: his very own family (Jacobs, 2018).

Emmanuel's story displays some of the simplest malfunctions in RAD children that can impact family life in significant ways. A child who has not experienced the most basic of normal interactions within a family will find even ordinary occasions like vacations and special days of the year, difficult to deal with. Often this will only become evident when such occasions crop up and it is important for parents of RAD children to keep in mind that such basics may be insurmountable obstacles for their children.

Chapter Takeaways

- Consequences for unwanted behavior must be clear and consistent.
- Consequences that you use for ordered children do not work with RAD children. Use specific RAD-focused consequences for your child to ensure they comply.
- Correcting behaviors in RAD children must also be done in a very specific way.
- Make sure that you have clear boundaries for your own reactions too.
- Pick your battles.
- Do not meet high emotion with equally high emotion.

Chapter 6:

Protecting Your Family

It can be really easy to slip into feeling all-consumed by the treatment of a RAD child. The other members of the household can easily be sidelined. As much as it is our responsibility to help the RAD child heal, it is also our responsibility to ensure that the rest of our family does not incur secondary trauma from that healing process. This is something that I struggled with in the beginning in trying to help my disordered son to heal, while still parenting my ordered child.

RAD children can be very difficult to live with and they can also pose a physical danger to others in the household. Despite the fact that your child has a disorder they cannot control, their behaviors, such as violent outbursts and physical attacks, can be defined as domestic violence. I know that is difficult to accept because of the associations with that phrase. It is true, though, and just as you would protect your children from domestic violence where a spouse is involved, you will need to do the same for the violence they witness and experience from a RAD sibling.

Living in a home with a sibling that may rage for hours or very suddenly become violent is frightening and can be emotionally and physically damaging. Just because your other children are not required to heal their RAD sibling, it does not minimize the impact the RAD sibling's violent outbursts have on them. Be sure to set aside time each day to talk to your ordered children and understand how they are feeling. Regular therapy sessions where they are taught coping mechanisms and have an outlet for their emotions can also be highly beneficial.

Although we don't want to think about this aspect of RAD, it must be said that children living with this disorder can be abusive toward their siblings. This can take the form of emotional, physical, or sexual abuse (Keri, 2019). Although you may not believe that your RAD child may be capable of this, it is vital that you keep an eye on this. It is part of your obligation as a parent. Your other children may not want to tell you about such abuse because they may feel like their RAD sibling will get into trouble or retaliate and the abuse will become worse. Ensure that your non-RAD children are aware that they do not have to accept any form of abuse or violence from their sibling, and that you are always open to hear their complaints or objections about such behavior without judgment or reprisal.

Have plans in place to prevent the escalation of RAD behaviors and protect your family. Ensure everyone in the family knows what to do in the case of such escalation. Such plans will make the rest of the family feel more at ease and in control. Plans can include other measures such as hiding all potential weapons, creating safe spaces for your non-RAD children, or surveillance equipment.

While CCTV cameras may not be ideal, they can be very helpful in keeping line of sight throughout the home. You can't be everywhere at once, of course, and in the case of any accusations being made, footage from CCTV cameras may be very helpful. An alarm on your RAD child's bedroom door may also be helpful in keeping track of their movements and ensuring they aren't moving around the home without your knowledge or supervision (Van Tine, 2020b).

Be sure that you have secured all dangerous objects out of reach of RAD children. This includes sharp objects, medications, and poisons. Sharp objects are more than just knives and, as we saw with a previous real life situation, includes seemingly harmless objects such as pencils (Van Tine, 2020b).

Designate safe spaces within the household where each member of the family can go if a situation escalates out of control. You can also agree upon a safe word that, when used, indicates to other members of the family that it is time for them to move to their safe space. Practice emergency plans with members of the family so that, when a heated situation arises, they already know exactly what they need to do without thinking about it (Van Tine, 2020b).

Of course, the severity of RAD differs from child to child and, for many families, involving law enforcement will never be necessary. For some families, situations can escalate to such an extent that you have no choice. Rather than be caught off guard, have a plan in place to contact the police when necessary. It is also important to have many different ways to make contact as, in the heat of a complex situation, you may not be able to locate your phone, it may be damaged in an incident, or you may be unable to speak on the phone. Other alternatives to contacting the police could be having a landline installed in a family member's safe space, installing panic buttons that are linked to the police station, or if you have several exits from the home, and it is safe to do so, have an older child go to a trusted neighbor to call police (Van Tine, 2020b).

When a RAD child exhibits behaviors that are unsafe to themselves or others, the role of the parent or caregiver as the protector is undermined. Law enforcement and social services may become involved. In some extreme cases, it may be necessary for the child to be hospitalized, removed from the home, or placed into a juvenile detention setting if the safety of the family is at risk.

Child-on-parent violence is not uncommon in homes where a RAD child is severely disordered and in such cases, it may be necessary to press criminal charges (Keri, 2019). This is not something that any parent or caregiver ever wants to do to their child, but sometimes, there is simply no other choice.

The Most Difficult of Choices

Although I am extremely grateful that I was never in this situation, I have been involved with many families that had to choose the safety of the rest of their family over having their RAD child in the home. This occurred in situations where the pace of treatment is greatly overwhelmed by the extreme and dangerous behaviors of the RAD child. I have witnessed the complete devastation of parents and caregivers forced with making this decision, but sometimes, it truly is the best thing for both the RAD child and the rest of the family. A situation like this may involve placing your child into a residential program, which at first glance appears to be little more than a holding cell, and sometimes it will mean having to lay criminal charges against the child. I have seen instances where residential treatment facilities have aggravated the RAD child's behavior, but very often these are still the best option to keep the rest of the family safe and also to protect the RAD child from themselves.

Image 12: Difficult choice

If you have had to make this decision, and your child has been living in a residential treatment facility for some time, it will be necessary to make preparations for their homecoming to ensure that a regression does not occur. Such preparations can include arranging for other children in the home to regularly spend time elsewhere such as sleeping over at trusted family members or attending playgroups. This gives the other child a break from the full-on intensity of living with a RAD sibling. Clear boundaries need to be set and communicated with the family, professionals, and friends before the child returns home. Bring someone along with you to collect your child.

Real Life Situation

When RAD children are little, it is easier to deal with their behaviors without outside intervention. When they become teenagers, and are stronger, you may have to make the difficult decision of calling in law enforcement for the safety of your child and yourself. The following is one mother's story of her interactions with law enforcement around her RAD child. Names have been changed to protect the identity of minors.

"What do you want me to do for you?" the police officer asked Jenny. She says that she will never forget the perplexed look on the young officer's face when she asked him to arrest her teenage son, John.

She tried to explain Reactive Attachment Disorder and how it changes the brain to the officer, but her explanation only confused him more.

The officer thought Jenny was crazy, along with everyone else. Most people have never even heard of RAD. Even those who have heard of it often have a hard time understanding it, unless they have lived with the disorder themselves.

Jenny and her family lived in a safe and stable community with caring first responders. It wasn't common to arrest 14-year-old kids for "petty theft," per their parents' request, in their neighborhood

Frankly, she says, she still felt a bit confused herself. As the officer stared at her, she asked herself how she got to that place in her parenting journey.

She still remembers the rush of relief when a therapist diagnosed her child with RAD. Although she knew very little about the disorder back then, she felt like they finally had something concrete. Their family had been drowning in John's physical aggression, lies, and manipulation. So when they finally had an official diagnosis that explained John's behaviors, she naively assumed that everything would be okay.

The first time Jenny and her family sought help from the police was in response to their son's new pornography habit. Although they knew John could not handle a cellphone or similar electronic device, they had bought him a Kindle Reader for Christmas. They didn't see any harm in it.

Within hours of receiving the Kindle, however, John had downloaded inappropriate books from the Kindle website. Jenny and her husband did what they thought was best and took away the Kindle for a while. They had a talk with him and they hoped that the pornography habit would stop.

When John started to access inappropriate websites on his friend's old cell phone, though, they realized they needed to do something more. That's when, per her friend's suggestion, Jenny reached out to youth services at the local police department. They had tried everything else up to that point, including lots of therapy and various parenting techniques, but nothing was working.

The officer Jenny spoke with seemed to understand. It was, to her surprise, a pleasant experience. He even sent an officer to her house to write a citation for her son to appear before youth services. The experience really seemed to shake John, and Jenny hoped this would be the wake-up call he needed.

A youth services officer sentenced John to 12 weeks of community service. He cleaned trash every Saturday and Sunday for three months. Jenny thought that she had found the solution to John's problem.

Every time Jenny picked him up from community service, he would gush about the great "friends" he had met that day. Most of the kids serving community service with him had criminal records.

Months after John's community service commitment ended, Jenny realized that she was missing several hundred dollars. She confronted John when he got home from school. He admitted, eventually, that he had stolen the money over the course of many weeks from his mother's wallet.

Jenny called the youth services department again, looking for help. The youth services specialist told her that they had nothing left to offer her family. Due to John's idolization of the kids in the group, community service was no longer a good option for him. She said that Jenny would need to have John arrested in order to get additional help.

Jenny was baffled. She could not believe that, as a society, we had to wait to react to a bad situation instead of proactively avoiding one.

Jenny says this is how she came to be the mom who stood on the front porch in her quiet suburban neighborhood asking the police to arrest her son.

Traumatized herself, she could not effectively explain RAD to the officer. She struggled to help him understand what it was that she needed from him. He even called for backup to help him figure out what to do.

Thankfully, Jenny's husband came home from work and backed up her story and reinforced her request that their son be arrested. The couple invited the officer into their home to speak with John.

Shortly after their son admitted to stealing the money, Jenny heard the clink of handcuffs. It is a sound that she never wants to hear again and a sound she will never forget. A sound of which the mere thought turns her stomach.

Jenny recalls the day feeling extremely slow but, in reality, it ended rather quickly. The officer booked John into the city jail and then called for his parents to pick him up a bit later. The whole ordeal lasted about six hours from start to finish.

The juvenile justice officers gave Jenny and her husband all they could within their guidelines. They at least helped her to provide John with logical consequences—an important parenting task especially for parents of children with RAD.

In an effort to learn more from their experiences and share knowledge with other parents, Jenny recently interviewed a police officer. She asked him what he would have wanted to know coming into the situation at their home that day. As a seasoned police officer and a seasoned mom of a child with RAD, the pair put together the following tips for parents.

The four best ways to get the police to understand your child with Reactive Attachment Disorder are:

1. Remain calm: Remember the primary task of first responders, per their title, is to assess for and diffuse immediate danger. It is only from there that they can start to gather information

The officer Jenny spoke with said that, when a parent is calm, he or she immediately relays stability and the potential to provide solid information. The calmer you appear, the more quickly and effectively you can get through to an officer.

2. Be honest: Tell the officer everything you can to help. If you feel embarrassed or hesitant, remember that officers encounter situations such as yours more often than you might know. We all do things out of fear or a need for protection at times, but remember that transparency helps the officer do his or her job, which leads to the next tip.

3. Let the officer do his or her job. Remember first responders need to follow specific procedures. Help the officer to follow protocol so you can get the right help as soon as possible. For example, an officer may need to arrest your child in order to transport and admit him or her to the proper psychiatric hospital. Or the officer may just need you to provide permission to take the child in. It all depends on the situation and where you live. Whatever the case, cooperate. Jenny had gladly agreed to press charges against her son because she knew it was necessary, albeit unfortunate, in order to get the help they needed. Only someone who has raised a child with RAD can fathom doing so, she knows, but she needed to do what was right for John.

To keep John from consequences would only aid his illness and prevent his growth as a person. And Jenny knew that, as a minor, the charges wouldn't follow him into adulthood. It was a small and helpful price to pay in the grand scheme of his life.

4. Prepare and practice. No concrete formula exists for exactly what to say when you call the police. Yet, you should prepare for your specific circumstances and child. As you do, come up with a short, concise explanation of Reactive Attachment Disorder that feels comfortable to share when the officer arrives.

RAD Advocates advises parents to include the following points when communicating with police officers:

- My child is dysregulated and is at risk of self-harm or harming others
- My child has been diagnosed with Reactive Attachment Disorder. It is a complex mental illness in which he or she may rapidly change behaviors,

especially when in front of strangers. Therefore, you may not witness the behaviors that I'm reporting.

- *The best way to support my child is for you to trust my report so we can unite in the best interest of him or her. I can provide you with the names and phone numbers of the mental health care providers with whom we work.*

- *After you prepare, practice, practice, practice. Rehearse it in your head and out loud. Even the most eloquent speakers get befuddled and tongue-tied in the middle of a crisis.*

- *Education about Reactive Attachment Disorder is scarce.*

Although it may feel daunting, remember above all that you are an educator in RAD. Jenny's interview shed further light on that fact. The officer said he didn't know anything about the disorder before he spoke with her. In fact, he had to research it online in preparation.

Like many other professionals, including therapists and educators, very few police officers receive training on RAD. It is up to parents, unfortunately, to fill that gap.

Armed with new-found knowledge about RAD, the officer reflected upon past situations with greater clarity. Some of his experiences had ended well, thankfully. Others could have turned out much better had he been trained on the disorder.

The officer left Jenny with the following anecdote about a situation that did end well.

A father, a former police officer himself, called 911 numerous times over the course of a week. Each time, he reported that his son had abused him. And each time the officer arrived at the scene, the son admitted to a physical altercation with his father. Yet, the father felt reluctant to press charges or allow his son to leave with the officer.

By the fifth call of that week, the officer told the father that he could not visit the home again and not do anything. He deemed the situation a domestic violence case and needed to act. He arrested the young man.

The father contacted the officer several months later and thanked him. As a result of the arrest, the son received proper psychiatric treatment and medications. He had never been healthier, said the father. Their home life was much better.

Jenny says that to call the police on a child is never a fairytale. It is often the first step and far from the last. Whether it is the first incident or one of many, it is not helpful to anyone, including the child, to minimize the harmful behaviors of a child with RAD.

Jenny's son is doing well these days. Due to the many hoops they had to jump through, he got the help he needed. Jenny does not regret the decisions that she had to make but she sure would not want to do it again.

"Sometimes the hard thing and the right thing are the same," said musician Isaac Slade. As a parent of a child with RAD, this is a mantra by which to live. It is not easy. There is no clear path, and it certainly isn't the path that most people tread. Parents need to lead their own way with the confidence that, for themselves and their children, it is right (Houze, 2021).

Jenny had to make, perhaps, one of the most difficult decisions a parent ever will. To turn your child over to law enforcement and put them at the mercy of a system you cannot control is devastating. In this case, it was probably the only choice she had. If she had let her son continue on this path without intervention, he likely would have found himself in far deeper trouble from a legal perspective.

Real Life Situation

I chose the following story to illustrate the dynamics that can be at play between an ordered sibling and a RAD sibling. Although this story refers to an adoption, the dynamics can be very similar in a biological situation too. Names have been changed to protect the identity of the minors involved.

Anita thought adoption would always be part of her future. She and her husband knew from the time they were married that they wanted to adopt a child someday. By the time their youngest daughter was about six-years-old, they felt the time was right.

Their family was healthy and close and everyone was excited about the adoption. Anita and her husband were given little to no advice about living with children with

RAD. Nor did they have an extensive history about the child they were about to embrace into their family. They simply assumed, with all the love they had to give, that everything would be fine.

Anita still holds a photo taken the first week their adopted daughter joined their family close to her heart. It shows their biological daughter holding hands with her new sister, Akisha, and walking down the hallway into school. Being in the same grade, their daughter by birth was thrilled to introduce her new sister to second grade. All four of Anita's children did everything they could to make Akisha feel welcome.

Anita says that the "honeymoon period" lasted about ten days. While Akisha seemed to settle into their home very quickly at first, her behaviors soon began to change. It began with displays of stubbornness and defiance. Akisha struggled with Anita, in particular, with accepting direction.

Anita thought that she just needed to hang in there until Akisha realized she was in a safe home and loved deeply.

They tried to give her all kinds of experiences with friends, sports, and school activities. Although Akisha seemed to thrive outside of their home, the battles continued to escalate behind closed doors.

Anita's youngest daughter became the main recipient of the physical abuse from Akisha. Akisha threw things at her, hit her, and pushed her. She said incredibly hurtful, spiteful things to their youngest daughter. Anita recalls feeling completely heartbroken. Anita thought that their daughters just had personality differences and they moved them into separate bedrooms to give them each more space. This only helped in giving a place to go during conflicts, and still, the tension continued to grow.

Anita felt that their home was no longer a refuge. She found it difficult just to get out of bed each morning to face another day. Her four other children were now spending more and more time isolating themselves in their rooms. They also left the house as much as possible. Anita felt that her family was falling apart.

After six months, Anita entered therapy for the first time in her life. She could not see how they would survive another month, let alone eight years before Akisha would be able to live independently. Anita remembers looking at the therapist through a flood of tears and telling her that the worst part was that she felt there was no hope. Despite their efforts to get support and guidance in their parenting, their relationship with Akisha continued to deteriorate.

About two years after Akisha joined Anita's family, she realized that Akisha was restricting her food intake. She was becoming dangerously thin and was in need of medical intervention. This was the beginning of a two-year cycle of hospital, home, hospital, residential treatment center, hospital. No matter how well Akisha did in the eating disorder programs, she refused to eat the instant she returned home. It was her way to get away from the family—back to another facility.

The more Anita and her family tried to support and nurture Akisha, the more resolve she seemed to have to restrict her food intake. It became impossible to keep her alive in their home.

When Akisha was ultimately diagnosed with RAD, all the behaviors finally made sense to Anita. It was incredibly hard to accept that their close family relationships, love and nurturing were too difficult for Akisha. Her early trauma had altered the way her brain had developed and she was in a constant state of survival in their home.

In order for Akisha to be safe, they needed to provide her a living situation without her triggers—the family. Anita eventually found Akisha a home specifically for children with RAD. In this home, she had no threat of love or nurturing. To her, that felt safe. She became more regulated and, in time, the food restricting subsided.

Anita says that she knows that theirs is not the adoption story people expect or want to hear. While she wishes their journey could have gone differently, it has led her to one of her life's missions and passions. She is now an avid advocate for families of children with RAD.

Certainly not all adoptions lead to a story like Anita's. Nor are all children with RAD adopted. No matter how these stories come to be, however, families of children with RAD need a voice and incredible support systems. Yet, they rarely have either. Anita says that she wishes she had known then what she knows now—that no amount of love from her family would have made Akisha's early trauma disappear. If she had known, perhaps they could have gotten her the right help early on. Maybe they could have saved their other children from the trauma they endured in their own home. Anita says that they were so hopeful that we could embrace Akisha and give her a family. Even though she cannot be in their home, she will always be in their hearts (Johnson, 2020a).

As Anita says, this is not the adoption story that the world wants to hear, but in this case, it was the way the story had to go. This is also an extremely interesting case study because it gives an example of a RAD child self-harming as her method of pushing the caregivers away. While there was an amount of violence toward her siblings, Akisha's physical behaviors predominantly focused on self harm.

Caring for Your Other Children

Possibly one of the most emotionally and physically exhausting things about parenting a RAD child is also having to ensure that you provide equal care, albeit in a very different way, for their siblings. It is easy to become caught up in the often all-consuming task of raising a RAD child and unconsciously allow your other children to see to themselves. This will only result in negative emotions from the other children though as they deserve attention and care just as much and they don't deserve to be sidelined by their disordered sibling. As you are developing your schedule for caring for your RAD child, be sure to carve out time each day that is specifically used to spend time with your other children. Try not to do this at the end of the day, where possible, as you will likely be exhausted from your efforts of the day, and your other children will not get an engaged and energized parent. Your other children are already going to be receiving far less time and attention than they would if their sibling did not have Reactive Attachment Disorder simply because of the intense, time-consuming nature of the illness and care required. This is why it is vital to be intentional about your care for your other children. Keep in mind that, although many forms of discipline and consequences may have little to no effect on your RAD child, everything you say and do will impact your other children, and often for the rest of their lives (Van Tine, 2020a).

I found that when I was able to think about my response to my son's behaviors as a teaching moment and advocate for the others in my home, my ability to handle such situations significantly improved. In helping to heal my RAD son, I was also able to teach my other child about the importance of justice and mercy.

Chapter Takeaways

- While you do your best to help your RAD child heal, do not allow the rest of your family to suffer because of it.
- Pay attention to the mental health of your entire family.
- RAD children can be abusive to their siblings too, not just their caretakers, watch for this as they are also extremely manipulative and may hide it well.
- Prepare for worst-case scenarios so that your family still feels safe in their own home.
- Understand and accept that you may have to make a choice between the safety of your family and keeping the RAD child in the home.
- Set aside time to spend with your other children and partners when the RAD child is not present.

Chapter 7:

Getting Help

There is absolutely no way that a family can deal with Reactive Attachment Disorder effectively without professional assistance. RAD is a serious disorder, and when not dealt with correctly, can result in devastating outcomes for both the child with the disorder and their family. Help can come from a variety of sources, but professional assistance is always the most important starting point.

Seeking Professional Help

When seeking the right professional help for your child, start with your pediatrician, an organization that specializes in RAD or child development disorders, or a child development specialist. You will need to find someone that will be able to work with you for a long period. It is far more beneficial to you and your family to work with the same practitioner for as long as possible. The practitioner will start to understand your child and their behaviors and will be able to suggest better and more effective individual treatments. You will also want to find a therapist that has experience working with Reactive Attachment Disorder. Not all practitioners specialize in the same areas and attempting to use a therapist that has more of a generalized focus will likely not have the same effect.

You may need to visit a few different therapists until you find one that connects with your child on an emotional level. Personalities play a role here too and just as we don't "click" with everyone, your RAD child will not automatically take to every therapist. Having a good emotional connection between the therapist and the child will help to improve their prospects of effective treatment.

Consistency and trust will be key in the relationship between your child and their therapist and will help to address the already existing issues of mistrust and abandonment in the RAD child (Smarter Parenting, n.d.).

Image 13: Psychiatrist

Real Life Situation

I struggled with whether I should include the following story in this book and, although, in the following chapter we will discuss success stories, I think that it is vital to also share the stories of what happens when a child does not get diagnosed and does not get treatment. I do not include this story to scare you, but rather to allow you to be fully cognizant of the reality of this disorder. Children living with RAD are tortured by their own disordered thinking and although they often take it out on others, sometimes, they turn it against themselves. Names have been changed to protect the identity of the individuals involved.

Theirs was a familiar story. Malcolm and his wife, Beth, turned to adoption in 1991. They thought surely there were millions of babies out there in need of two loving people desperate to be parents. Then they learned about the realities of adoption. A foreign adoption seemed their best bet, but options were limited then. To improve their chances, they would need to be open to an "older" or "special needs" child. This was not how they had envisioned starting a family, but they wanted to be parents.

A chance encounter with another adoptive family steered them to an adoption attorney in Warsaw, Poland. Beth was of Polish descent and spoke the language. Maybe this was their chance, the couple thought. In a late night phone call to Warsaw from their home in Connecticut, the attorney was sympathetic but discouraging. She had a long backlog of clients and available children were scarce. What about an "older" or "special needs" child, Beth asked. It was then that they first heard about a 14-month-old girl in a rural orphanage. In a matter of five short months, they had rushed through home studies and background checks before boarding a flight to Poland to receive their daughter, whom they had named Catherine. It was nothing less than a miracle.

Catherine was an unwanted pregnancy, a three-pound preemie whose twin sister had been stillborn. She went straight from the delivery room to an incubator to an orphanage in Mragowo in Poland's northern lake district. At 14 months, she was withdrawn, listless, unable to sit, crawl, or feed herself. Medical records were scant. To Malcolm and Beth, she was perfect; nothing that two able bodied Americans couldn't fix with love, they thought .

In the years that followed, it seemed that a loving home was all Catherine needed. They moved from Connecticut to the San Francisco Bay Area where she transformed into a bright, spirited, charming little girl.

In the privacy of their home, though, things were often different: violent tantrums, uncontrollable crying, and defiance became the norm from little Catherine. Malcolm and Beth looked for answers from friends, pediatricians, therapists, counselors, and pastors, but were assured repeatedly that Catherine was just high-strung; she would grow out of it. In the meantime, the couple just had to be tough with her. Though fully aware of her abandonment and adoption, the professionals never explored the matter.

At 17 years old, Catherine gained early admission to Bennington College in Vermont with a bright future ahead. She wanted to make a difference in the world.

But she never made it.

Just five months shy of her high school graduation, she took the keys to her parents' car, drove to the Golden Gate Bridge and jumped.

Drowning in grief, Malcolm and Beth looked for answers. How could this have happened? What did everyone miss? What could they have done differently? They went to the library and scoured the Internet for everything they could find on adoption, something they had never thought to do before. They learned about Reactive Attachment Disorder and how it can have a devastating effect on orphaned children. It explained everything: the angel at school and the tyrant at home, the tantrums, crying jags, low self-esteem, and defiance, things that she kept carefully hidden behind a suit of armor from parents, therapists and friends.

How could everyone have been so blind, the couple marvelled?

They connected with other parents of children adopted from foreign orphanages and heard similar stories. Some stumbled onto appropriate treatments whereas others, like Malcol and Beth, were left in the dark. Adoption and attachment experts shared therapies and parenting techniques that have proven effective in dealing with the unique emotional needs of orphaned children. This information was in the public domain, yet everyone involved in Catherine's short life missed it.

The couple acknowledge that they can't have another Catherine do-over. She was one of a kind, but regardless of the tragic outcome, Malcolm and Beth always considered themselves the luckiest people in the world to have been her parents for 16 of her 17 years.

From her death, they learned that adoptees can be exposed to disorders that are still misunderstood by many professionals. Not every adoptee has attachment issues, but for those who do, treatment can be elusive.

The couple says that other adoptive parents who may struggle with what they did can use their story as a learning experience. Malcom says that parents should acknowledge their child's loss, parent her in a way that may not be intuitive to you, and get her the right kind of help. Just "loving her enough" may not be enough.

Hopefully, he says, that will save a precious life (Brooks, n.d.).

Catherine's story is heartbreaking and perhaps we will never know if RAD treatment and parenting techniques would have stopped her suicide. As Malcolm says, though, if there is anything that can be taken from this tragic loss of life, it is that adoptive parents need to be well informed and given support. If just one person had mentioned the words 'Reactive Attachment Disorder' to Malcolm and Beth, that may have set the whole family on a completely different path. Reading stories like this makes me all the more set in my decision to continue advocating for RAD children and their parents. I believe that the RAD conversation needs to be had with every couple considering adoption and more medical professionals need to be looking for the sign at wellness checks. Not just with adopted children, of course, but with biological children as well.

Treatments and Therapies

In my experience, early intervention is most certainly key to improved outcomes in children with RAD, so before we even discuss treatment and therapies, it is important for us to understand that, even if we vaguely suspect our infant may be dealing with the onset of RAD, professional help must be sought immediately.

While RAD can be a frightening and chaotic disorder, treatment is possible, and even in the most severe of cases, committed and consistent work with a professional can make an enormous difference. With treatment, children with RAD can be taught to develop healthier and more stable relationships with parents, caregivers, and others. This will help to provide models for relationships in life ensuring that your child is able to have healthy adult relationships too.

The ultimate goals of treatment are to ensure that the child has a stable and safe living situation, they develop positive interactions, and strengthen attachments to caregivers and parents. It's important to acknowledge that much of the treatment for RAD is going to focus on you as the parent or caregiver. You will need to be open to that in order to help your child. You are a key component in their healing because their disorder and behavior predominantly revolves around you.

Treatments and therapies for RAD can include:

- **Psychotherapy or psychological counseling:** a mental health practitioner will work with the child and caregivers or parents in a wide variety of ways. Sometimes this will be on-on-one and sometimes as a group. This form of treatment is geared toward building skills and reducing negative behavior patterns.
- **Family therapy:** this form of therapy involves working with the primary caregiver or parent and the child to help develop methods of healthy interaction.
- **Play therapy or social skills intervention:** this is usually used with younger children and teaches them how to interact more appropriately with other children of their age in normal social situations.
- **Cognitive restructuring:** this is a form of Cognitive Behavioral Therapy (CBT). Cognitive restructuring helps the RAD child to learn that negative thoughts such as, "I'm lonely," or "I am not loved," can be reinterpreted and reshaped. These thoughts can be changed to more logical thought patterns such as, "I feel lonely right now," or "I am having the thought that I am not loved." This helps the child to understand that the thought they are having is not necessarily the reality and may, in fact, be as a result of their disorder. Cognitive restructuring will give the child the tools they need to start interrogating their own thoughts and understanding the reality rather than the clouded emotion of their disordered thinking.

- **Special education:** RAD behavior patterns can significantly impair opportunities for learning. This presents an ongoing challenge for the child as they are not only struggling in the moment, but any possible future is being damaged incrementally as well. School-based programs do exist which can help RAD children to gain new skills and succeed socially and academically. In such programs, they will be taught by qualified professionals trained in teaching children with behavioral difficulties.
- **Caregiver or parent skills classes:** this is, of course, aimed at giving parents the skills and techniques they need to effectively and successfully raise RAD children.. This is something that I found very helpful as, in the beginning, I truly felt lost in a mass of information. I really needed someone qualified to guide me in the best way to handle certain situations.
- **Caregiver or parent education and counseling:** this is therapy aimed at helping you to emotionally deal with the strains of raising a RAD child. For a long time, I wanted to believe that I did not need help with this, but I eventually realized that for parents of RAD children, self care is vital. If you don't take care of your own emotional and physical health, you will not be able to properly care for your RAD child or the rest of your family (Mayo Clinic, 2017b).

There is currently no medication for Reactive Attachment Disorder itself. Medical professionals may, however, be able to help your child with some of the symptoms of RAD such as insomnia, explosive anger, or anxiety (Mayo Clinic, 2017b). This will be done by using medications designed to be used for those individual symptoms. By doing so, you can help to increase the success rate of overall RAD treatment as you deal with some of the difficulties, you create a more balanced environment for healing.

Resources for RAD Children and Parents

Healing a RAD child is a community effort. The RAD community, and its resources, can be found in various places. Besides your medical team, there are a few online resources that I highly recommend to help you in your RAD healing journey.

Attachment.Org

Find it at: https://attachment.org/parents/links

About the resource: Attachment.org is an online community that provides resources to parents, educators, and therapists to help work with children with various forms of attachment disorders including RAD.

Reactive Attachment Disorder Support Group on Facebook

Find it at: https://www.facebook.com/groups/1071879796263505/

About the resource: This online support group for parents, caregivers, and others living with the consequences of RAD is intended to be a safe and easily accessible space for you to share and get advice from those that are dealing with the same challenges.

RADadvocates.org

Find it at: https://radadvocates.org/

About the resource: RAD Advocates is a nonprofit organization. The organization is made up of people that have firsthand experience parenting children with RAD. The members have faced the intense difficulties that often come with RAD and understand the lack of resources available to support families and children. The members of RADadvocates all felt isolated and alone until they found their way to what they refer to as a "secret, underground" world of RAD families. These parents and caregivers found understanding and support with families that were facing similar issues, and they could connect and learn from others' experiences. Members of RADadvocates believe that the disorder must be brought to the forefront to help increase awareness and to get help to those affected so that they can receive proper treatments and interventions. They believe that these children and families deserve the same opportunities for treatment as those with other medical conditions.

Instituteforattachment.org

Find it at: https://www.instituteforattachment.org/

About the resource: The Institute for Attachment and Child Development (IACD) provides a holistic resource for RAD children and families including treatment as well as placement opportunities with trained foster families to ensure the successful treatment of RAD children. The IACD will also help to reintegrate RAD children into the home environment after treatment has occurred outside of the home.

Support Group for RAD parents on Adoption.com

Find it at: https://adoption.com/rad-support-group-for-parents

About the resource: This resource helps to guide parents and caregivers in locating a RAD support group in their area and one that will meet their needs and make them feel comfortable. There is often nothing more empowering than being surrounded by people that truly understand the challenges you are dealing with. Often, it is not even about getting solutions, it is more about not feeling alone.

Raisingdevon.com

Find it at: https://raisingdevon.com/resources-for-parents/

About the resource: Raising Devon is an online resource aimed at helping parents and caregivers to raise children with behavioral disorders.

Cautions Around Seeking Help

Image 14: Caution

As I mentioned when we discussed the myths around RAD, when it comes to treatment, you will very likely come across some less-than-effective, and questionable methods. Although I am a huge advocate of support groups for RAD parents and caregivers, I must admit that, it was also in these groups that I found some of the strangest and most dangerous advice. As long as you use support groups solely for support and not treatment advice, they are hugely valuable, but do beware of taking any treatment advice there.

This is, of course, not the only place that unhelpful and dangerous treatment advice for RAD exists. As with any disorder or challenge, a range of dangerous treatment methods have sprung up for RAD over the years, and it is important that you do not fall into these traps.

Some examples of dangerous treatments are pseudoscience treatments, such as attachment therapy or rebirthing methods. These pseudo-treatments are dangerous and have resulted in the injury and death of several children (Schwartz, n.d.). Many of these pseudo-treatments make the mistake of assuming that if an attachment is created, it will heal the trauma that had led to the development of RAD. This is not correct and forcing the development of attachment will actually lead to more problems in RAD children. Properly researched RAD treatment instead focuses on healing the trauma so that attachment can eventually be possible. Forming an attachment is therefore not the starting point of treatment, but rather the hopeful end point (Schwartz, n.d.).

When seeking a psychotherapist, be careful who you choose. Do not be shy about asking to see a license and proof of experience. There will always be people, and professionals, that believe their indirect experience, education, or opinion is sufficient to treat children. This is not certainly not the case with RAD children who need experienced, professional help.

Chapter Takeaways

- You will need professional help in healing your RAD child.
- Be careful about how you select the professional you use and ensure that they are trained to deal with attachment disorders.
- There are various treatments and therapies available for RAD children. The one that works for your child may be completely

different from another child. Trial and error is often the only way to determine which will work.

- Be prepared to be a major part of your child's healing.
- There is a growing pool of resources for parents of RAD children. They can sometimes be difficult to find, but they are there if you look hard enough.
- Do not fall into the trap of pseudoscience treatments that will only do more harm than good.

Chapter 8:

Staying Sane

Your child relies on you to help them heal and, as much as you focus your time and attention on their treatment, it is also important that you care for yourself. The old adage, "you cannot pour from an empty vessel," could not be more true than with caregivers and parents of RAD children. The ongoing and consistent challenges we live with can truly drive us over the edge if we let it. It is for this reason that I am dedicating an entire chapter to ways that you can help to maintain your own emotional health. This, of course, applies to your partner and family too.

Image 15: Challenges

Parenting a RAD child can be a lonely, overwhelming, uncomfortable, humbling, and exhausting journey. Often, the most important part of caring for yourself is accepting that it is not your fault. Even if something that you did contributed to the development of your child's RAD, it is very likely that you did not do that on purpose, and you certainly would never have dreamed that your child would develop a lifelong disorder.

Children with RAD are victims of a mental disorder that they did not ask and you did not cause. Even the most patient and clear-minded of caregivers will be challenged by RAD behaviors. It is important that you try not to give in to the depression and discouragement that will often develop from the challenges you face (Institute for Attachment and Child Development, n.d.).

Education about RAD is a phenomenal starting point as knowledge really is power. Understanding exactly what you and your child are experiencing will make the process easier. Proper knowledge and understanding of what is going on in your child's head will be valuable to the entire family. The RAD child will also appreciate being surrounded by people that make an effort to understand their disordered thinking and relate to them in comfortable ways (Institute for Attachment and Child Development, n.d.).

Find someone that you trust to care for your child so that you can occasionally have a break. As consistency is so important in a RAD child's life and, often, inconsistent caregiving is the very cause of the disorder, this needs to be done carefully. Ideally, you will want to use the same alternate caregiver on each occasion that you need a break so that the child is used to them. Also try to make the break part of your routine, but don't do so in a way that the RAD child can use this to create chaos by planning negative behaviors when they know you won't be there. Select a caregiver that is familiar with RAD and able to cope with the negative behaviors.

Get into the habit of practicing stress management activities on a regular basis. This can include meditation, yoga, and exercise activities that you enjoy. Just as your RAD child needs a release for their pent-up emotions, so do you.

Just as you are making time for your family, you need to make time for yourself. I very quickly became completely wrapped up in caring for my RAD child and lost myself. It took some time and conscious work to find myself as an individual again and redevelop my own interests. The amazing thing was that, when I did start to find my own space in the world again, I actually became a better parent. I had a lot more physical and emotional energy to give. Be sure to surround yourself with emotionally rejuvenating things, and that will be different for everyone. Something as simple as a nap, a glass of wine, a warm bubble bath, a massage, or a pedicure can make all the difference in refilling your emotional tank (Institute for Attachment and Child Development, n.d.).

You will need to acknowledge that you are not going to always be okay. There will be times in your journey with your RAD child when you feel frustrated, angry, hopeless, and helpless. This will happen and it is okay. The key is to find a way to pick yourself back up again so that you can continue with your child's healing and, ultimately, your own.

As you work your way through this journey, be sure to be kind to yourself. You are doing the best that you can to navigate a journey that you likely never have before and probably never thought you would. Parenting is difficult enough when your child does not have RAD, you are doing the best you can in a really tough situation. There will be times when you feel like you are a failure and, when that happens, you need to be ready to assure yourself that you are most certainly not. You are an advocate for your child and you are a resilient and strong fighter.

It is very difficult for a parent not to feel an affectionate bond with their child. It can feel completely unnatural, but such is the nature of RAD. It's a disorder that neither you nor your child asked for and all you can do is make the best of the situation and work toward healing. It is vital that you are able to forgive yourself for any mistakes you have made in the past. Hanging onto them is not going to do anyone any good. Learn from your mistakes and do your best not to repeat them (Van Tine, 2020a).

There will be occasions when you do not react the way that you know you should, but you cannot take too much responsibility for your child's negative behavior. Remember that even the most perfect of parents (if such a thing exists) would struggle to be gentle and calm when faced with the type of behaviors that a RAD child presents with and brings into the home.

There may be times when you will need to consider respite care for your RAD child. Respite care is when qualified people care for your RAD child so that you can take a break, care for yourself, and parent at your best in the long term. When your RAD child presents with particularly severe behaviors, respite care may be the best option to allow you to rest, rejuvenate, work on your marriage, and your relationships with your other children. Even though you love this child, their disorder will force you to need a break from them occasionally for the good of the entire family unit. When choosing a respite carer, be sure that you select someone with knowledge of RAD and also someone that is willing to follow your instructions and do what is best for your child. A respite will not be one if you are still worried about your child, so you will need to make arrangements that ensure you can rest and not be concerned.

This is certainly not a journey you can travel on your own, and a robust support system is key to success. Families of RAD children will need extended family, friends, neighbors, and others to support and surround them and learn about developmental trauma so they may help when needed. Figure out who in your support system can be called upon in times of need and who will not judge you or your family harshly. An experienced therapist will be a vital part of your support circle as they will help you to work through the emotional conflicts that parenting a challenging child presents. Support groups with other parents of RAD children can also be really beneficial so that you can find friends that really understand what you are going through.

Common Situations that May Lead to a Parent's Breakdown

Therapists, the parent's spouse or significant other, and extended family members see only a well-behaved and likable child with an angry, unfair, and unreasonable parent. They issue unwanted and unhelpful parenting advice that feels condescending and, as a result, the parent feels even more angry and depressed.

Caretakers, extended family members, and other adults feel bad for the child because they are not seeing what the primary parent is seeing and do not understand RAD. They give the child whatever they want. The child acts out even more with the parent so as to increase time with those that support the negative behaviors. The parent starts to avoid childcare opportunities because the child is more entitled and difficult afterward. The respite of this break is lost and the parent becomes more overwhelmed.

Image 16: Child holding parents' hand

Friends may make excuses to avoid getting together with the parent who is exhausted and complains a lot about her life with the child. The parent may also make excuses not to visit family or friends because they don't believe or understand them anyway and being around them leads to more pain.

The continuous defiance and opposition from the child and lack of support from outside parties begins to wear the parent down. They start to give in to the battle that feeds the child's entitlement and a vicious circle is born. The parent feels as though they are failing (Van Tine, 2020a).

In the parent's pursuit of a solution, they may find only expensive out-of-home options. They may begin to feel resentment toward the mental health care system and professionals.

The parent is required to constantly supervise the RAD child for their own protection, as well as the protection of them, and other children in the home. The parent becomes exhausted from the need for constant hypervigilance. A feeling of hopelessness, and helplessness pervades, and the parent may struggle with sleep issues.

The parent may feel resentful towards the RAD child. Their temperament is challenged and the parent feels that they have become a person they never wanted to be.

Real Life Situation

The following story illustrates the major effect that raising a RAD child can have on the life of the parents. Just as it is vital to care for your RAD child's needs, it is also equally important to care for your own physical and emotional needs. It also highlights how, even the most seemingly qualified of parents—those with psychology degrees and experience of their own—can still be completely overwhelmed by RAD.

Sabrina says that she has held a front-row seat to the "trauma chronicles" since she and her husband adopted their son 11 years ago and since she sustained a life-changing injury of her own.

Sabrina and Greg adopted both of their children from overseas, and she says that the unfortunate reality is that every adoption story begins with the trauma of abandonment. This initial trauma can predispose children to an increased vulnerability to everyday stressors, such as holidays and increased responsibility. Things that could be considered typical for most families.

In addition, their son spent the first 28 months of his life experiencing extreme neglect, malnutrition, and abuse in his orphanage. The couple suspects that he was kept alone in his crib for hours at a time, as he had virtually no rudimentary language skills, he recoiled from human touch and eye contact, and he lacked muscle tone to keep his body from toppling over in a seated position. They also saw that any swift movement toward him would cause him to lift his hand in a defensive position. This was concerning, but certainly nothing they couldn't handle with awareness and sensitivity—or so they thought.

Sabrina and Greg both have degrees in mental health and school psychology. They felt that if anyone could parent a child with a history of trauma, neglect, and abuse, they could. Plus, their daughter had proved to be a hearty soul, and they hoped that she would be a great role model for their son. Sabrina describes her bloodhound-like tenacity to seek out early intervention and resources, her husband's expertise, and their daughter's delightful, humorous personality, and says that she felt that these things would surely bring their son up to par in the world, where he would hopefully thrive one day.

Yet despite all of her efforts, Sabrina's son pushed her away. In the early days, he would throw his head back, regardless of what dangerous protrusion might be behind him, or turn his head to the side to avert having to look into her eyes. He held a perpetual scowl and darkness behind his eyes, seeming to prefer being in another world somewhere—anywhere besides with a family attempting to love him.

Trauma is everywhere, Sabrina says. It is physical for some and emotional for others. Trauma does not discriminate, but it can educate.

Sabrina remembers the time her son tried to push her parents' new kittens down the stairs and lock them in a box. She realized at that moment that he really did need constant supervision to avoid hurting himself or other living beings. He just did not seem to inherently care about anything.

Fortunately, Sabrina and Gred had the financial resources and the foresight to know that their child would require specialized interventions, and that they would need a village to help him.

Still, she says, it can be difficult to keep up appearances. Nevermind the reality they were living at the time, secretly hiding their loneliness and depression as they raised a child who they had deep concerns about, and who was difficult to connect with.

From a "typical" parenting perspective, there is nothing "normal" about raising a child who has experienced trauma, Sabrina says. It is completely and utterly counterintuitive, and this does not even take into consideration that resources are virtually nonexistent for parents who find themselves in their situation.

As the ruggedly independent, strong person Sabrina was, she attempted to swallow her loneliness and carry on. She took her son to medical and applied behavioral analysis therapy appointments and maintained as "normal" a family life as she could.

She did all of this until a split-second distraction landed her in the hospital. She suffered a climbing fall that, she says, was more than likely due to her own pent-up stress and anxiety. Even a severely fractured ankle, pelvis and back did not immediately funnel her thoughts toward her own well-being. While waiting for the paramedics to arrive, she continued to direct folks toward calling the several appointments her son would be missing because of her "little mishap."

Sabrina has since read many articles alluding to the secondary post-traumatic stress disorder some parents face when they have children with disabilities or additional needs. She now knows and can acknowledge exactly how real that is.

When serving on the Family Advisory Committee for Children's Hospital of Wisconsin, Sabrina became friends with other parents who faced similar struggles: isolation, depression, hypervigilance, fatigue, and desperation. Parenting a child with additional needs can be an all-encompassing, life-defining endeavor. Most people don't end up in the hospital, however, but she did. That's the thing about parenting, Sabrina says, you just carry on.

Two years, 11 limb-salvage surgeries, and three hospitalizations later, Sabrina ended up losing her leg below the knee. Folks rallied to help her family as she recovered, including grandparents, friends, therapists, their church community, and people from their kids' schools. Sabrina would regularly send them information from her bed, trying to educate everyone about how to work best with her child and to understand how the mind of a child of trauma operates. They have been fortunate enough to have caring, compassionate people along the way. She says that it has been hard, but she has learned so much.

Life can be beautiful and awe-inspiring. It can also be painful and treacherous. There is a saying, "You never have to apologize for how you choose to survive." As a young mom parenting a child of trauma, Sabrina says, this often involved retreating to the basement, blasting Alanis Morissette, and curling up in a ball to cry (as well as cracking open a beer at noon on occasion).

Survival strategies for her son and many others like him often include coping mechanisms that can be harmful or destructive. It can be easier to isolate, bury feelings through substance use, zone out in front of the TV or social media, or even hurl violent comments or images at others than it can be to look deeply into the eyes and heart of another human being.

Retired teacher, David Blair, recently wrote an open letter in which he pleaded with students to put down their phones and make friends with kids who eat lunch alone. Sabrina says that she agrees, wholeheartedly! She also feels that we really need to do a better job of supporting parents and caregivers of kids with disabilities or additional needs. Obviously, this road is not easy. It does take a village, and Sabrina feels that we need more real villages these days, not just the ones online.

Sabrina has a message for the "trauma mamas" and other parents out there feeling alone and isolated: pay attention to the stirrings of your own heart and any difficulties you may be carrying. Own them and work through them. Reach out to others to share and ask for help. As hard as it may be, don't let the super-parent persona take over, or the perfection façade of social media keep you from connecting with others. She says that she is a prime example of how trauma can happen when you don't connect and ask for help. Real, open human connection is what it is all about.

Six and a half years have passed since Sabrina's accident, during which time the family has been forced to slow down a bit. She has not been able to "do it all," which, in retrospect, she knows, has been a blessing.

Her husband had to share some of the kid-appointment responsibilities because she has acquired some appointments of her own. Quality time spent with family and friends became golden. It isn't easy to accept help, much less ask for it, but the lesson she learned in having caring people step forward in her life has been priceless.

Slowing down has also taught her to listen with her ears, eyes, and heart. When her son's behaviors are out of control, she looks into his eyes and sees fear. Fear of not being good enough or not being in control. It is no coincidence, she says, when she notices these feelings come full circle to bite her in the butt. Touché, she thinks. Slow thyself down. Connect.

She often thinks about what would have happened if she had talked about her struggles prior to her accident, and if she had paid attention to her own well-being. Trauma begets trauma, she learned. The antidote? Mindful awareness and connection.

Sabrina's family has learned so much and grown in ways she would never have imagined. Her once resistant son does his homework right after school. He has a good friend and is learning to be a good friend. He even snuggles with our cat and feeds him every day. He is learning the value of connection. They have weathered the storm, she says, and continue forging on. There are always new things to learn.

"Compassion is the radicalism of our time," the Dalai Lama once said. Sabrina believes this to be revolutionary and true. Trauma will continue to be a regular occurrence unless we make human connection intensely personal. We need to be present, and to learn from one another with all that we are.

We need to understand the generational trauma that some people continue to carry and help unpack it in ways that truly open our hearts and minds. If we do, Sabrina thinks the reward will be not only immediate, but it will affect generations for years to come (Prange-Morton, 2018).

Image 17: Sad child

Chapter Takeaways

- You cannot pour from an empty cup. Take care of yourself so that you are present and able to take care of your RAD child.
- Raising a RAD child is taxing on both an emotional and physical level.
- Secondary Post Traumatic Stress Disorder is not uncommon in parents of RAD children.
- Understand that the situation is not your fault.
- Be kind to yourself.
- Consider respite care as an option if you need to.
- Work on building a robust support system.

Chapter 9:

There is Hope

As difficult as this journey is and, although it can sometimes feel like you are making no progress, be assured that there are thousands of children with RAD who have grown up to be well-adjusted adults. With the right treatment and consistent application of RAD parenting methods, your child can grow up to have deep, long-lasting relationships with friends and family.

Image 18: Happy family

In wrapping up this book, I wanted to share some success stories with you, because I want you to know that it is entirely possible for your child to heal and live a fulfilled life. By applying the techniques I have shared in this book, building a support system, and consistently working with your RAD child, you can help them to heal.

Success Stories

The following are real stories taken from online postings. Names have been changed to protect the identity of those involved.

Melanie and Saskia

Melanie adopted her daughter, Saskia, from Russia when the child was six years old. Saskia was defiant and non-compliant from the second day in Melanie's care. Her behavior quickly escalated into high-level aggression. Saskia hit, kicked, bit, spit, and everything in between. Melanie started Saskia in therapy before she was even fluent in English, but it didn't help. Other therapists and psychiatrists didn't help either. In between the hell, Melanie saw glimpses of a funny, smart, creative, and athletic child.

Eventually, Saskia was diagnosed with Reactive Attachment Disorder. For a while, she struggled to find an attachment therapist, but eventually, found one that knew her stuff. For a while, it got worse as Saskia fought against the treatment. Then, slowly progress happened, alternating with lots of backsliding. Melanie learned to parent Saskia in new ways and she worked on all of her emotional baggage. When the child's aggression flared, she went to therapeutic respite where she practiced being respectful and did chores. After 16 months of therapy, Saskia was attached and compliant, with no more aggression.

Saskia is now 19 and just finished her first year at university.

Melanie describes the process as "horrific." She lost her business and many friends, and came to the edge of bankruptcy.

She says that while there was nothing easy about what she went through, the result is beyond wonderful (Johnson, 2020c).

Melanie's story is one that I can relate to from my work with families with adopted children. The language barrier in this case would have created even more difficulties. The struggle that Melanie went through is one of the main reasons that I wanted to write this book. I do believe that, today, Saskia would have been diagnosed a lot more quickly. Adoption agencies and social workers are a lot more aware of RAD behavior and can help parents to find the correct help sooner rather than later. Depending on the country that you adopt from, it is important to realize that you may not always get accurate information about your child. The situation that the child was living in pre-adoption may not have been ideal and may have added to already existing trauma. When adopting internationally, I advise parents not to take anything at face value. Record keeping may not be as accurate as it is in the United States, and your child may suffer if you assume the information you've been given to be true. Rather, assume the worst at all times and seek assistance for your child immediately if any symptoms of RAD start to present. In this case, symptoms were presenting on the second day in Melanie's care, yet due to circumstances, it still took some time to get Saskia the help she needed.

Sarah and Milton

Like most parents, Richard and Sarah made their children, thirteen-year-old Mark and 10-year-old Michael their top priority. They took parenting seriously, and other moms often turned to Sarah for parenting advice. When a family friend decided she wanted to adopt a child, she told Sarah she thought she would be the ideal person to help with babysitting.

Within months, Sarah's family friend had been matched with an adorable five-year-old little boy named Samuel. As planned, Sarah babysat regularly. Just three months later, though, Sarah's friend called her again with astonishing news. She said that she didn't want Samuel anymore and was calling a social worker to have him removed. They were so close to transitioning from foster care to adoption. Appalled and saddened, Richard and Sarah decided that someone needed to do the right thing. After all, Samuel had already been in five different homes within the space of 13 months.

Sarah asked if they could adopt Samuel. Three days later, Richard and Sarah had completed all the necessary paperwork, fingerprinting, background checks, and home visits. Two social workers planned for Samuel to stay with their family while the paperwork was being processed.

Samuel didn't seem at all concerned during this time. He behaved like any other five-year-old little boy. Six weeks later, past parental rights had been terminated and Samuel was officially placed in Sarah and Richard's home.

When his social worker told Samuel that Richard, Mark, Michael and Sarah were his new family, he was excited and immediately asked if he could have a 'M' name like his brothers. Ten months later, on a warm summer day, Richard and Sarah officially adopted Samuel as Milton.

The transition for Milton, while seemingly easy at first, soon began to unravel. Of course, Sarah and Richard figured it was to be expected and were prepared for what they believed would be a rocky, but short-lived, transition period.

When Milton started kindergarten, Sarah began receiving calls from the school to pick him up. He was disruptive in some way or another. The school eventually stopped asking Sarah to pick him up after a while, however, as the occurrences were just too frequent, and they felt Milton needed class time in order to succeed academically. Instead, they would call Sarah at home or discuss the day after school. The talks about behaviors always went well in front of Richard or the teacher and Milton seemed to want to learn how to behave correctly.

When Milton and Sarah were alone, though, he acted very differently than he did with other adults, even Richard. He was withdrawn, sneaky, and defiant. He also lied regularly. Sarah tried to discuss Milton's troubling behaviors with Richard and her parents, but they said that Sarah was being too hard on Milton. They said that she should learn to let some things go. Frustrated but determined, Sarah tried her best to back off and try a different approach.

Time passed but matters grew worse. By the summer of second grade, Mark began having problems with his new brother too. Sarah started to notice how Milton purposely caused Mark to get in trouble. When she reprimanded Mark, Milton watched from afar with a sly smile.

One mid summer day, though, Sarah felt like they had made a breakthrough. It had been a long day of struggling with Milton's behaviors. Tired but hopeful, Sarah tried to just sit with him and sort out his feelings. Surprisingly, Milton began to share some things about his past. Sarah did her best to comfort and reassure him that Richard, the boys, and her were always going to be there for him.

That evening Michael and Mark went to a friend's house. Sarah decided to take Milton to their neighborhood pool—just the two of them. The walk there together was quiet and calm for a change and Sarah was feeling positive about the outing. They got to the pool, put down their things and got into the water. Sarah recalls thinking how nice it was to spend time together that day.

Milton proudly wanted to show Sarah how he could tread water in the deep end and she joined him and praised him for his swimming skills. They began playing around, laughing and splashing in the pool as the sun warmed their faces. Then, Milton swam behind Sarah, and pushed her beneath the water with all of his strength. As Sarah tried to push to the top of the water for air, Milton pushed her back down again and again. Sarah was suddenly terrified, gasping for air, flailing to get away, and fighting for her life. After several minutes, Sarah got free and climbed out of the pool. Coughing and crying, she yelled for Milton to get out of the pool, but he swam away from her instead.

When she went to the other side of the pool to get him out, she stepped on a rock and felt instant pain. Sarah had broken her foot. She called Richard, hysterical, and yelled to Milton to go to a friend's house nearby.

Sarah returned from the hospital hours later in a boot cast. Mark and Michael ran and hugged her, but Milton stayed back and watched from a distance. Still in shock, Sarah could not pinpoint exactly what had happened, but she definitely knew that she had been attacked by Milton.

When Richard asked Milton what had happened in the pool, he said that he was slipping and tried to hold onto Sarah in the water. With nothing concrete, the culprit simply became the rock.

Days later, the friend who had stayed with Milton the evening of the accident came over. She asked if she could talk to Sarah alone. Sarah's friend told her that Milton had said that she had hit him and showed her bruises.

Sarah defended herself by explaining that those bruises were from his skateboard and scooter, not from her. Sarah's friend was not entirely convinced, saying she knew that they had been struggling with the child and that she wanted Sarah to know that Milton had told many people that his adopted mother was hitting him. Sarah was dumbfounded, angry, and confused. Sarah had no idea, at the time, that she was living with Reactive Attachment Disorder.

As the summer progressed, the family continued to fall apart. Although Sarah did not realize it at the time, Michael and Mark felt as though they needed to protect her from Milton's abuse. In their eyes, their dad had failed to do so. Meanwhile, Milton abused and attacked Mark regularly as well. Mark stayed in his room much of the time and rarely socialized with the family. Friends had also stopped calling and coming around and Sarah's mother would not talk about any of it with her. She felt completely isolated.

Milton continued to struggle at school and was not excelling academically. He also had been caught stealing from a classmate and forging his dad's signature on a school paper. After many rejections for more help from the school, Sarah ultimately decided to homeschool Milton.

What followed was an incredibly difficult year. Sarah constantly felt defeated and incredibly confused by Milton's behavior. No matter what the subject, he struggled with every single assignment she gave him. He would argue over everything incessantly, all day and Sarah was exhausted. As soon as his father got home, though, Milton completed his assignments immediately, correctly, and quickly. So, of course, Richard could not fathom Sarah's frustration.

Sarah eventually felt a gleam of hope when she found a child psychologist who seemed reliable. She ultimately diagnosed Milton with visual and language processing disorders. The psychologist used a computer program especially to meet Milton's needs and impairments—to help him break through the places he was struggling and "rewire" his brain paths. Milton went to the psychologist every day for a year. At the end of the computer program, the psychologist retested his brain and deemed the intervention successful. Milton could return to public school for the fourth grade, she said.

Milton's behaviors hadn't changed at all, though, and Sarah had caught him multiple times lighting matches in the garage near gas cans. She found him trying to light a marble on fire on the carpet of his bedroom. None of these behaviors were displayed around Richard. Nonetheless, Richard and Sarah planned on returning Milton to public school, and she felt hopeful that he would at least succeed academically.

A few weeks into school, Milton's teacher still said he wasn't working to his full potential. They stayed the course and discussed an individual education plan. Sarah desperately needed those few hours while he was in school to herself each day.

One warm day in May, Sarah received a phone call from a social worker. Milton's biological mother just had a baby and the county wanted to keep the siblings together. The social worker asked if Richard and Sarah would pick up Milton's sister from the hospital in the coming days. Initially, the couple declined to help. They were already going through enough with Milton. Later that same day, though, they realized that this child had not been harmed by the birth family. She had not even left the hospital yet and they might be able to prevent whatever Milton had experienced so they called the social worker back and agreed to take the baby girl.

At the time, Sarah and Richard had no idea that the baby was in the neonatal intensive care unit detoxing from methamphetamines. Her mother had taken drugs regularly throughout her pregnancy and even up until three hours before giving birth. There would be no way of telling the effects that drugs, stress, and homelessness had in utero on the baby until months later.

The day they brought the baby home, Richard and Sarah told Milton that he and the baby shared the same birth mother. He lit up and said, "I have someone now." They were happy for both of them and hopeful that the kinship would help Milton. Within a year, they officially adopted the baby girl and named her Melissa.

Throughout fifth and sixth grades, Milton had many accommodations afforded to him in school. He always had extra time to do his work and get extra help, yet, he still failed nearly every subject because he refused to utilize these accommodations. Sarah found piles of homework, completed but laying on the floor in the back of his closet—never turned in. At the end of the sixth grade, Sarah questioned how the school administrators could let Milton go onto the seventh grade when he had essentially failed the fifth and sixth grades. Once again, she decided to homeschool him. That year, Milton began acting out even more destructively. He destroyed nearly everything that Mark and Sarah valued. Sarah caught him cleaning the toilets with her toothbrush. She found him filing down a flat-head screwdriver to, as he put it, make a shank. He told her that he carried a knife in his pants.

Sarah struggled to comprehend how all this was happening yet no one else saw or believed it. She reached out to their post-adoption social worker for some help or respite, and was flatly told that they had no services available to them after adoption.

Sarah decided to find a therapist for Milton and herself. After just a few visits to her therapist, Sarah was diagnosed with complex anxiety, post-traumatic stress disorder, and depression. The therapist suggested medication and journaling. Several months into Milton's therapy, his therapist showed a video that Sarah thought explained Milton's behavior. The video briefly explained something called Reactive Attachment Disorder. Milton had 18 of the 20 characteristics of the disorder. Sarah was flabbergasted.

The therapist diagnosed Milton with RAD due to his early childhood abuse and neglect. The therapist and Sarah began working together to research the best way to treat the disorder. Even she didn't know what Milton needed at that point, but at least they had a diagnosis that seemed spot-on. The chaos that Milton had brought to the home, though, had only escalated.

As Sarah searched for the best way to help Milton, she found several "underground" RAD groups on social media—parents who privately support one another virtually, judgment-free. She quickly joined them and, for the first time, did not feel crazy. Like Sarah, these parents of children with RAD felt blamed and shamed by everyone—from their own parents to their children's teachers. She learned that, sadly, it is a common problem.

Sarah learned that RAD is considered rare and is wildly misunderstood. Parents of children with the disorder typically feel alone and can't find effective help for their families. The parents online led Sarah to more resources and information. She learned that she was the "nurturing enemy" to her son—a term that only a parent of a child with the disorder could fully understand.

It made perfect sense as she reflected on the last few years. Essentially, a child who has experienced early trauma pushes away the caregiver who attempts to get closest to him or her emotionally. She realized that nothing good was to come from Milton being with her, his "nurturing enemy" all day, every day.

Milton returned to public school after months of homeschooling. This time, though, Sarah was armed with the knowledge of his disorder and how it looked so different in public than it did at home. She educated his teachers and the school administration about how we could all work together for Milton's success. They were receptive and, for the first time in years, Milton began working at grade-level.

Just as Sarah and her husband felt as though they were starting to "get it", however, their daughter Melissa began having grand meltdowns. The child had screaming fits that lasted for hours. Melissa scratched, punched, and slapped Sarah and no one else.

As Melissa and Milton were biological siblings, Sarah wasn't completely shocked by her behaviors. After all, it surely wasn't new to her. She was devastated to begin reliving the same things she had dealt with in Milton. She felt like she was starting all over again.

Just as the summer before the eighth grade ended, Milton began to relapse as well. Sarah's son Mark, returned from college to the room he shared with Milton only to find that Milton had been urinating under the bed. He had also stolen or destroyed many of Milton's personal belongings that were stored in the closet. Suddenly, the family was again in complete crisis.

Then Sarah uncovered Milton's pornography addiction and his inappropriate social media behavior. Eighth-grade proved to be much of the same—theft, defiance and destruction.

At this is the point Richard really started to see the big picture. He realized that Sarah's inability to sleep at night for fear of attack from their son may be founded after all.

The family installed cameras and door alarms inside and outside of the house. They called the social worker again, but no one would help. By the end of eighth-grade, Milton had been arrested for theft and served 12 weeks of community service. Feeling hopeless and helpless, Richard suggested relinquishing their parental rights. At least Milton could get mental health care from the state and they would be protecting their family.

The couple turned to social media groups for help and they were directed to RAD Advocates, a non-profit group founded by mothers of children with Reactive Attachment Disorder who help other parents. The guidance they received from RAD Advocates changed their course dramatically. Armed with confidence and concrete information, Sarah called the social worker again.

The social worker suggested placing Milton in a group home, but Sarah knew this would not help his actual issues and may indeed make things worse. Through RAD Advocates' guidance, Sarah found an alternative therapeutic residential program that could work specifically for Milton.

It took a great bit of push and persistence, but Sarah prevailed with the guidance of RAD Advocates. The social worker agreed to help get Milton into the program. The day came when Milton left home to begin the program. The clinicians projected he would return home in 12 to 18 months. At the time, Sarah was not sure that would be long enough. Meanwhile, she began searching for therapists who specialize in RAD for Milton's return home, and after lots of research and many phone calls, she finally found one.

Sarah met with the therapist and explained all that had happened with Milton and Melissa. Sarah felt particularly confused about Melissa's behaviors as they were so similar to Milton's behaviors, yet, she was most definitely attached to their family which was so different from Milton. After several sessions, the new therapist diagnosed Melissa with complex trauma.

During that time, more pieces of the puzzle were coming together from Milton. A part of his therapy in the program was to make amends with his family. He apologized for specific situations and things that he had done. He even admitted trying to drown Sarah that day at the pool and that he had been mean to Melissa. Sarah learned that Milton had unknowingly repeated his cycle of abuse onto Melissa. He had spent the greater part of Melissa's life mentally, psychologically, and emotionally abusing her. He had trained her to cause chaos and abuse in their home in the same way he had.

While everyone agreed that Milton was making great progress, Sarah was devastated and bewildered at his admissions, and she shared with the therapists that she did not feel as though Milton should return home. Sarah did not feel ready, and she didn't feel as though she could keep Melissa safe.

For many months, the family worked on healing and learning more about the disorder. They focused on changing their mindset and redirecting their anger from Milton to the disorder itself. Milton also agreed to help the family "fix" what he had done to Melissa.

Seven months after leaving home, Milton returned from the program. From there, they continued to work intensively with their hometown therapist at least once a week. Milton was finally revealing the hurt and sorrow underneath his behaviors all those years, and Sarah saw the adorable brown-eyed, curly-headed little boy that had come to live with them so long ago.

At the time of Sarah sharing her story, Milton had been back home for nearly a year. Their lives are drastically different from how they had been living over the past decade.

Milton has a part-time job and is completing high school. He is calm and engaged with the family in a healthy way. Of course, he still has a teenager's attitude from time to time, but it is nothing compared to what it used to be.

Melissa is thriving, and she continues to learn how her brother's "sick brain" taught her the wrong things. She is learning how his "well brain" is helping her too. Melissa had a great kindergarten year.

Milton and Sarah have a safe and joyful relationship now. They share looks and giggles over inside jokes. He is even able to poke fun at himself about his past behaviors. Laughter and fun fill the house.

Sarah feels incredibly grateful for her family, but she would not wish the decade of her life on anyone, and that is why she is now a part of RAD Advocates herself. She hopes that her experiences can lead at least one family to the training, education and resources they found. Sarah can only imagine the pain and damage her family could have avoided if they had the help they needed sooner.

Sarah says that if she could share only one piece of knowledge about living with Reactive Attachment Disorder, it is this—love and time are simply not enough, but there is hope to be found (Houze, 2020).

I was hesitant to include Sarah's story here, as it is rather disturbing, but I think it is a fair, honest, and realistic representation of what RAD can do to a child and their family. Many of the behaviors we see in this example are typical of RAD. We note that Milton's aggression and resentment was initially centered on his mother and then on one of the family's biological siblings. He then turned his behavior on his own biological sister as well. The fact that Sarah, despite being a full time mom and emotionally present as well, did not know about the abuse toward Melissa by Milton, is testament to the manipulative and secretive nature of RAD.

This story also provides us with an example of how the schooling system (initially) and even the social services system can work against parents with RAD children and not provide them with the resources they need. I think one of the biggest lessons we can take from Sarah's story is that, once the family were able to get the right diagnosis and put Milton on a structured path of treatment, they saw excellent results. In their case, they had no choice but to have Milton treated outside of the home and I personally think they did the right thing. There is nothing more difficult than sending your child to live outside the home and acknowledging that you alone, do not have the skills to heal him, but sometimes it is necessary.

This story also gives us a frightening example of how children with RAD can turn on their caregivers in public and make false accusations of abuse. Milton did this so convincingly that even Sarah's friend was unsure as to whether she was telling the truth or not. This is an aspect of RAD that makes treating the child extremely difficult. We are honed to believe a child when they accuse adults of abuse and, in most situations, rightly so, but the evidence must be carefully looked at in all cases of such claims.

I have no doubt that both Milton and Melissa will go on to live full and fulfilling lives and be able to form deep and long lasting relationships in the future. Had these children not landed up in a home where the family was committed to their care, though, their story may have ended very differently.

Another reason that I was a little hesitant to share this story is because, I fear, that it paints the adoption process poorly and may make people less likely to adopt children. I want to be clear that not all adopted children come with issues like this, and RAD can just as easily happen in cases of biological children, as was the case with my own family.

Dina and Maxine

Dina's pediatrician could not have been more pleased with Maxine's progress. At 18 months, her baby was gaining weight perfectly. She was walking and talking, and her muscle tone was good. These were all excellent indicators of progress for a child she had adopted just 14 months earlier from an orphanage in Siberia.

Image 19: Blond baby

Dina's paediatrician specialized in treating internationally-adopted children. During her daughter's third scheduled check-up, the doctor recommended another round of vaccines because he did not trust the ones the baby had received in Russia. He asked Dina how Maxine was eating, and she told him she was on an organic, whole-food, non-meat diet. The doctor approved of this and told Dina she was doing a great job, and that Maxine should return when she was six months old for another check up. As the doctor started to leave the room, Dina stopped him and asked whether he could tell her how she would know if Maxine was okay from an emotional perspective.

Dina explained to him that her precious blonde daughter, an exceptionally radiant child, did not cling to her or look her in the eye or even tolerate being held. She did not reach for Dina's hand, let her read to her, or play with her. Dina told the doctor that her baby was a little "manic," unsure if that was even the right word to describe it. She went on to describe Maxine as being restless when she was restrained in a stroller or crib. She never relaxed into an embrace and was controlling and difficult all of the time.

Without missing a beat the doctor told Dina that she could be describing something called Reactive Attachment Disorder. RAD, as Dina would later discover, is common in adopted babies, particularly from Russia and Eastern Europe where their social services systems are overloaded and children are not given individual attention from birth. Dina came to understand that babies have difficulty attaching to their adoptive parents because they have been neglected, abused or traumatized, and they see the adoptive parent as just another unreliable caretaker who could possibly abandon them. Even though they are so little, these infants believe that the only ones they can trust are themselves. Dina would discover that this is a complicated condition, that is generally not well understood by many pediatricians.

Dina's pediatrician said that it may be too early to diagnose as Maxine was very young.

Both Dina and her husband were 40 when they adopted Maxine. Dina was a writer and her husband was a retired lawyer. Never during the entire adoption process did anyone mention RAD to them. She first heard it mentioned when they were in Siberia. Another couple who had been adopting their second child at the same time expressed concern when they met their new son because the child did not make eye contact and was unresponsive to their attempts to connect. At the time,

Dina did not know enough to pay attention to their concerned reaction. She heard the condition mentioned again when speaking to a family friend, a psychotherapist, but this friend had been talking in broad strokes, and gazing down at Maxine, and then quickly brushed it off saying the toddler looked fine.

Even after her pediatrician's mention of the syndrome, Dina was prepared to accept this explanation, though it would have explained why she was feeling so inadequate as a mother. It would take another two years, when Maxine was four and gaining a command of language, for her husband Bob and her to make it their life's work to understand RAD, and to do what they needed to do to rescue their daughter from the isolated place she was trapped in.

Specifically, it took a bad day at a nursery school concert to take the first step that was needed to turn their lives around. During a recital, Dina broke down and sobbed because she realized how lonely and displaced and isolated her daughter was. Maxine was unable to sing along with the group. Her extremely disruptive behavior forced an educator to take her off the stage. This may not sound like the most unusual of occurrences for a young child, but put in context, Dina understood in that moment, that she needed to intervene.

Dina and her husband worked together to read everything in medical studies, books, and online that they could on the disorder. So many of the symptoms matched up with RAD that Maxine seemed to be the textbook example of a RAD child. They made a dogged effort and a conscious commitment to help their daughter and make themselves into a family. It was their daily work. They came to understand that raising a child who has trouble bonding requires counter-intuitive parenting instincts—some that disturbed and concerned family and friends. People could not understand when they would respond to Maxine's fussing with a passive, expressionless face rather than indulge her. They would laugh during her tantrums until she abandoned them, and then moved on as though they had never happened. they had to do this because RAD kids are addicted to chaos and it's crucial to take away the drama. Outsiders didn't understand that Maxine wasn't willing to give hugs and they didn't ask her to do so. With the help of case studies and research, they were able to develop a tool box. Some advice they received was invaluable, and some advice failed. Some techniques worked for a short while. They often felt like they were living inside a laboratory. Dina knew how lucky she was to have a partner like Bob because so many homes and relationships are ravaged by the challenge of adopting difficult children.

Over time, engagement with Maxine improved and increased in frequency. It wasn't necessarily warm and loving at first, but it was moving in the right direction. They were drawing her out. She became better able to show her anger rather than indifference. As her verbal skills developed, they had the advantage of being able to explain to her verbally that they loved her and would never leave her. They could explain that they understood how frightening it was for her to be loved by an adult and that she was safe. They taught her how to feel at ease when they looked her in the eye, and trained her to do the same. Understanding how hurt she was also opened Dina's heart and made her more compassionate, and more motivated to be Maxine's mother.

Progress took some time. The work of staying bonded with a disordered child is a life-long endeavor. Maxine stepped out of the danger zone when she was about five or six. She shook off her armor and helmet and allowed Dina to become her mother. Dina says that she honors that trust by remembering, each and every day, how she struggles with subconscious demons and how enormous her battle is and will always be.

At 11 years old, Dina is amazed by Maxine. She says that it's not just her witty sense of humor which enables her to draw sophisticated cartoons or the way she is playing the violin or doing well in school. Her greatest accomplishment is allowing herself to be loved. While that is second nature for most families, for their family it is a major triumph (Traster, 2014).

Dina and Maxine's story is an excellent example of an early diagnosis and how vital that can be to healing. They were extremely fortunate to be seeing a doctor who, having dealt with adopted children before, was able to identify the possibility of RAD in the infant. Although it would take some time for Dina and her husband to come to grips with the fact that RAD was indeed having a major impact on their daughter and their family, when they began in earnest to gather information about the disorder, they were quickly able to accept that their daughter needed professional help.

Another aspect of this story that is interesting is how Dina and Bob's friends and family reacted to how they parented Maxine. While the couple seemed happy to ignore their concerns, it could be helpful to sit them down and educate them around RAD and the specific parenting techniques required to deal with it. This would make both the couple's and the friends and family's life a lot easier.

Having been diagnosed at an early age, Maxine was able to heal relatively quickly and she now has better prospects than ever at a full recovery.

A Study Aimed at Identifying the Efficacy of Early Intervention in Children with RAD

The following is less personal than some of the other success stories, but I wanted to include it because it is a clinical study conducted with 10 families and gives us a really good group effect to look at. I also think that group studies are helpful to look at, because when we look at individual instances, it's easy to feel that other people's lives are very different from ours and perhaps their success will not be ours. When we look at a group, it is much easier to believe that, at least one of those families, must have similar dynamics to ours.

The study was conducted by James Drisko, PhD, at the Smith College School for Social Work.

The purpose of the study was to examine responses from adoptive parents, child welfare workers, and treating clinicians and to determine what intervention methods lead to marked progress in children with Reactive Attachment Disorder (RAD). Working with these children bridges child welfare, mental health practice, and schools and these are all key areas of social work practice that need a stronger evidence base. A research report by O'Connor and Zeanah stated that there is no empirically supported effective treatment for RAD. There are no Cochrane (or similar) systematic reviews on RAD and very limited empirical study on this disorder beyond single case studies so further exploratory/formative work is indicated (Drisko, 2005).

The method of research used in this study was as follows: Ten families of children with RAD who had been assessed by child welfare workers or clinical social workers to have made considerable and enduring progress were nominated for in-depth study. The children ranged from seven to 22 years of age at the time of the interview. Initially, all the children had difficulty trusting, emotional constriction, peer relationship issues, and seven of the children had PTSD symptoms. Families consented to two semi structured interviews to identify what factors led to this progress. Further, their child welfare workers and clinicians were each separately interviewed, providing triangulation and additional perspectives. Probes explored specific strategies leading to progress and identified strengths. Responses were analyzed using the Glaser and Strauss constant comparative method and organized using ATLAS.ti software. Strong inter-coder reliability was established, peer reviews helped identify omissions and biases, member checks insured the analysis reflected participants' views in a valid manner (Drisko, 2005).

The results of this study were as follows: Gains shown by these children included deepened familial relationships, better control of moods and behavior, improved ability to articulate feelings, better peer relationships, academic progress and decreased PTSD symptoms. Ten core categories were developed. Parents attributed these gains to several factors which center on areas of special strength evident in these families. Parents made a strong initial commitment and bond. Parents persisted in the face of many challenges to develop true attachments over several years. These parents all kept a positive outlook. In terms of daily life, parents were always available, physically, visually, or aurally. Parents provided a highly structured living environment, similar in many respects to a residential treatment center. Parents also employed behavioral management techniques of many kinds and were able to quickly appraise their effectiveness and appropriate use. Psychologically, parents showed remarkable ability to be intersubjectively attuned to their child despite confusing cues and behavior. Parents maintained a balanced appraisal of their child, finding strengths while noting limitations. Parents were able to both seek out and to effectively use social supports (family and informal and formal supports). They encouraged their children to be involved in peer activities even when problems emerged and they had to serve as coaches and consultants to group leaders. Progress was notable, but did not completely overcome the effects of profound early challenges (Drisko, 2005).

The implications of this study were found to be as follows: Even allowing for retrospective recall bias, this study extends the available knowledge base regarding interventions for RAD. Findings affirm and add to the available case study literature. Findings also outline a tentative treatment package for future prospective study (Drisko, 2005).

The findings of this study are really important because they emphasize the need for consistency and structured environments in the lives of RAD children. It also shows the major importance of the parent or caregiver in the treatment plan, and how healing cannot occur without a caregiver or parent that is completely on board.

Chapter Takeaways

- RAD does not have to be the end of your hope for a fulfilled life for your child.
- Therapy does work when applied consistently.
- Celebrate small wins all the time.
- Success is defined differently for every child and each family. Embrace your success daily, even if it doesn't look like everyone else's.

Conclusion

Writing this book feels like both the end of one journey and the beginning of another. From the moment my son was diagnosed with Reactive Attachment Disorder, I have wanted to share our story. My story is slightly different from those that you have read in this book as Craig is my biological child and the cause of his RAD was something quite unavoidable. Of course, I would have no idea when I sat in the psychiatrist's office that day and heard the term 'RAD' for the first time that this disorder, and others like it, would become my life's work.

Life is funny that way, I've found. Just when you think you are in the deepest, darkest valley of your life, the path is being built for something bigger and better. You just have to be willing to walk the path.

Image 20: Path

The knowledge I have shared with you in this book is an accumulation of personal experience, academic research, and personal stories from the life of others. I do want to be very clear that this book in no way replaces the professional counsel of qualified therapists and psychiatrists. It is a resource, much like support groups, institutes, and counselors that you will find along the way on your RAD journey. I do hope that it will be a valuable resource to those that come across it.

Loving and raising a child with RAD is very likely the most difficult thing a parent will ever do. It is a situation that will force you to put everything you think you know about being a good parent on the back burner and instead become a caregiver. In giving this care, again, we cannot do so in the way we instinctively feel best. If we want RAD children to heal and thrive, we have no choice but to care for them in the way they need to be cared for.

If there is one word I would assign to being a parent of a RAD child it is: humbling. There will be very few situations in life that will force you to completely cast aside your ego, the way caring for someone whose disorder detests the sight of you, will. You will survive it. Even though all of your instincts are screaming at you, you will overcome this if you stay the course.

In the beginning of this book, I briefly touched on the issue of medicating RAD children. While there is no silver bullet in chemical form for this disorder, there are medications that will allay some of the symptoms such as insomnia and anxiety. Some families do find that treating these symptoms with medication help to provide a more stable emotional base upon which to build the treatments for attachment disorder. If this works for you, that's great. If it doesn't, don't feel compelled to medicate your child to comply with demands from the outside world. Throughout this journey, you will need to make many difficult decisions, whether to medicate or not is just one of them. The safety of your child and others in the household is the most important factor to consider. Don't make decisions that will put anyone at risk or push ideals that you will regret later.

If you are currently the parent of a child that displays many (or any) of the symptoms I have mentioned in this book, I implore you to seek out a qualified attachment therapist and get your child assessed. Please do it right now. As you will have read in this book, with RAD children, time is of the essence and early diagnosis can be the difference between healing and years of struggle.

If you are reading this book because your child has just been diagnosed with RAD, I hope that you now have a deeper understanding of what your child is experiencing. Please do not stop with this book alone. Although I am proud of the resource I have put together here, it is far from all encompassing and there is so much more for you to learn. Knowledge truly is power and with RAD the more you know, the better equipped you are to figure out the path ahead.

If you have read this book simply because you have an interest in attachment disorders, I salute you for your interest. Please now go and help to advocate for children and parents with this disorder so that we may begin to help them all heal.

Before I sign off, I would like to touch on the topic of fostering and adoption. Many of the stories we have read here involve adopted children with significant behavioral issues. I do not want this to put anyone off adoption, but I will tell you that it takes a very special family to adopt. Please go into an adoption journey with the understanding that you are not going to bring a child into your family and magically have them integrate without any issues. That is simply not realistic. Even if the child has not been abused, there will always be a transition period. Please, if you can, stay the course. These children desperately need you.

I would like to think that there will come a day when children are no longer victims of abuse and neglect, but I fear that, if that is even possible, we are a long way off. We cannot change a child's past, but we most certainly can change their future.

I wish you all the strength, power, and knowledge that you need to help your RAD child heal, and may your story be among those of success.

I truly hope that you have found value in this book. If it has changed even one life, my goal is accomplished, but I would love for it to change even more. If you would like to become an advocate for RAD children and ensure that more parents get the help they need, please be sure to leave a review on Amazon so that more people can find this resource.

References

American Psychiatric Association. (2013). *Diagnostic and statistical manual of mental disorders* (5th ed.). https://doi.org/10.1176/appi.books.9780890425596

Brooks, J. (n.d.). *Home.* Www.iheartcasey.com. http://www.iheartcasey.com/Blog/Home.html

Christian Homes and Special Kids. (n.d.). *What's it like to parent a child with Reactive-Attachment Disorder (RAD)?.* https://www.chask.org/adoption/birth-parents/whats-it-like-to-parent-a-child-with/whats-it-like-to-parent-a-child-with-reactive-attachment-disorder-rad/

Cleveland Clinic. (2018, August 21). *Reactive Attachment Disorder: Causes, Symptoms & Treatment.* https://my.clevelandclinic.org/health/diseases/17904-reactive-attachment-disorder#management-and-treatment

Del Luca, M. (2013, July 10). *Kid Confidential: What Reactive Attachment Disorder Looks Like. Leader Live.* ASHAWire. https://leader.pubs.asha.org/do/10.1044/kid-confidential-what-reactive-attachment-disorder-looks-like/full/

Discovery Mood & Anxiety Program. (2019a, August 23). *Children with Reactive Attachment Disorder (RAD): What's Next?.* https://discoverymood.com/blog/reactive-detachment-disorder-children-with-rad/

Discovery Mood & Anxiety Program. (2019b, June 12). *Common Myths About Reactive Attachment Disorder.* https://discoverymood.com/blog/common-myths-reactive-attachment-disorder/

Drisko, J. (2005, January 14). *Success Stories: Identifying What Works in Treating Reactive Attachment Disorder.* Sswr.confex.com; SSWR. https://sswr.confex.com/sswr/2005/techprogram/P1428.HTM

Elevations RTC. (n.d.). *Common Myths About Adoption and Attachment Disorder in Teens.* https://www.elevationsrtc.com/common-myths-about-adoption-and-attachment-disorder-in-teens/

Houze, H. (2020, March 11). *A story about a mom, adoption and the reality of living with reactive attachment disorder.* Radadvocates.org. https://radadvocates.org/blog/a-story-about-a-mom-adoption-and-the-reality-of-living-with-reactive-attachment-disorder

Houze, H. (2021, January 13). *When a parent needs to call the police on her child with reactive attachment disorder.* Www.radadvocates.org. https://www.radadvocates.org/blog/when-you-have-to-call-the-police-as-a-parent-of-a-child-with-reactive-attachment-disorder

Institute for Attachment and Child Development. (n.d.). *Connie's Story: What it's like raising a child with reactive attachment disorder.* https://www.instituteforattachment.org/connies-story-what-its-like-raising-a-child-with-reactive-attachment-disorder/

Jacobs, K. (2018, June 21). *What trauma did to our kid.* Medium. https://medium.com/the-plan-b-vibe/what-trauma-did-to-our-kid-70f6c5ee12bf

Jean. (2016, August 15). *Our Journey with Reactive Attachment Disorder.* No Hands but Ours. https://www.nohandsbutours.com/2016/08/15/journey-reactive-attachment-disorder/

Johnson, K. (2020a, February 20). *Adoption, children with reactive attachment disorder & family; Expectations vs Reality.* Radadvocates.org.

https://radadvocates.org/blog/childrenwithreactiveattachment disorder

Johnson, K. (2020b, February 24). *Why It's Not Your Fault Your Child Has Reactive Attachment Disorder.* Radadvocates.org. https://radadvocates.org/blog/why-it-s-not-your-fault-that-your-child-has-reactive-attachment-disorder

Johnson, K. (2020c, July 1). *Why we made the heart-wrenching decision to send our child to "RAD boarding school".* Radadvocates.org. https://radadvocates.org/blog/why-we-made-the-heart-wrenching-decision-to-send-our-child-to-rad-boarding-school

Keri. (2019, May 24). *Parents of kids with RAD: 10 Unfortunate truths you must know.* Raising Devon. https://raisingdevon.com/2019/05/24/parents-of-kids-with-rad-10-unfortunate-truths-you-must-know/

Mayo Clinic. (2017a). *Reactive attachment disorder - Diagnosis and treatment.* https://www.mayoclinic.org/diseases-conditions/reactive-attachment-disorder/diagnosis-treatment/drc-20352945

Mayo Clinic. (2017b). *Reactive attachment disorder - Symptoms and causes.* https://www.mayoclinic.org/diseases-conditions/reactive-attachment-disorder/symptoms-causes/syc-20352939

Nicole. (n.d.). *When people don't get it: Raising children with reactive attachment disorder.* Institute for Attachment and Child Development. https://www.instituteforattachment.org/when-people-dont-get-it-raising-children-with-reactive-attachment-disorder/

Prange-Morton, C. (2018, June 28). *What It's Like to Parent a Child With Reactive Attachment Disorder.* The Mighty. https://themighty.com/2019/06/childhood-trauma-reactive-attachment-disorder/

Renee, J. (n.d.). *RAD: Behavior and Consequences.* Every Star Is Different. https://www.everystarisdifferent.com/2015/06/rad-behavior-and-consequences.html

Smarter Parenting. (n.d.). *Reactive Attachment Disorder (RAD)*. https://www.smarterparenting.com/behavioral-issues/reactive-attachment-disorder-rad/

Smith, M., Robinson, L., Saisan J., & Segal, J. (2019, March 21). *Reactive Attachment Disorder (RAD) and Other Attachment Issues*. HelpGuide.org. https://www.helpguide.org/articles/parenting-family/attachment-issues-and-reactive-attachment-disorders.htm

Schwartz, A. (n.d.). RAD: *Children, False Information and Dangerous Therapies - Childhood Mental Disorders & Illness, Child Emotional Problems*. MentalHelp.net. https://www.mentalhelp.net/blogs/rad-children-false-information-and-dangerous-therapies/

Traster, T. (2014, May 1). *A Story of Adoption and Reactive Attachment Disorder*. Psychology Today. https://www.psychologytoday.com/us/blog/against-all-odds/201405/story-adoption-and-reactive-attachment-disorder

Van Tine, A. (2020a, March 30). *Post Page*. Radadvocates.org. https://radadvocates.org/blog/a-reactive-attachment-disorder-parenting-guide

Van Tine, A. (2020b, April 17). *6 Things to Know When You First Learn Your Child Has Reactive Attachment Disorder*. Radadvocates.org. https://radadvocates.org/blog/6-things-to-know-when-you-first-learn-your-child-has-reactive-attachment-disorder

Van Tine, A. (2020c, December 29). *Post Page*. Radadvocates.org. https://radadvocates.org/blog/a-woman-s-dreams-of-adoption-and-a-fight-for-her-family-s-safety

WebMD. (2020) *Reactive Attachment Disorder*. https://www.webmd.com/mental-health/mental-health-reactive-attachment-disorder#2

Image References

Image 1: *Happy Children* (n.d.). https://pixabay.com/photos/children-siblings-brother-sister-817365/

Image 2: *Baby* (n.d.). https://pixabay.com/photos/people-bed-baby-newborn-child-1839564/

Image 3: *Frightened child* (n.d.). https://pixabay.com/photos/boy-lonely-asian-sad-alone-child-4658244/

Image 4: *Screaming child* (n.d.). https://pixabay.com/photos/scream-child-girl-people-kid-1819736/

Image 5: *Adopted child* (n.d.). https://pixabay.com/photos/adoption-love-mother-and-child-177427/

Image 6: *Scared child* (n.d.). https://pixabay.com/photos/scream-child-girl-people-kid-1819736/

Image 7: *Mischievous child* (n.d.). https://pixabay.com/photos/naughty-boy-sweet-face-cute-4117665/

Image 8: *Children being affectionate* (n.d.). https://pixabay.com/photos/children-hug-siblings-brother-920131/

Image 9: *Practicing good behaviors* (n.d.). https://pixabay.com/photos/siblings-brother-sister-children-817369/

Image 10: *Consequences* (n.d.). https://pixabay.com/photos/child-kid-play-study-color-learn-865116/

Image 11: *Rating behaviors* (n.d.). https://pixabay.com/photos/feedback-survey-nps-satisfaction-3709752/

Image 12: *Difficult choice* (n.d.). https://pixabay.com/photos/sadness-tears-crying-sorrow-no-joy-4578031/

Image 13: *Psychiatrist* (n.d.). https://pixabay.com/photos/doctor-patient-consultation-5710152/

Image 14: *Caution* (n.d.). https://pixabay.com/photos/spooky-halloween-ruins-2813134/

Image 15: *Challenges* (n.d.). https://pixabay.com/photos/holzfigur-stones-life-struggle-980784/

Image 16: *Child holding parents hand* (n.d.). https://pixabay.com/photos/people-man-father-baby-kid-child-2605835/

Image 17: *Sad child* (n.d.). https://pixabay.com/photos/portrayal-portrait-crying-cry-baby-89189/

Image 18: *Happy family* (n.d.). https://pixabay.com/photos/family-people-child-smile-2811003/

Image 19: *Blond baby* (n.d.). https://pixabay.com/photos/angel-baby-beautiful-blond-child-17045/

Image 20: *Path* (n.d.). https://pixabay.com/photos/forest-path-sunset-sunlight-way-166733/

Made in the USA
Monee, IL
04 March 2022

92264145R00089